HEGEL, HAITI,

and Universal History

Susan Buck-Morss

UNIVERSITY OF PITTSBURGH PRESS

Published by the University of Pittsburgh Press, Pittsburgh, Pa., 15260
Copyright © 2009, University of Pittsburgh Press
Manufactured in the United States of America
Printed on acid-free paper
10 9

Library of Congress Cataloging-in-Publication Data

Buck-Morss, Susan.
  Hegel, Haiti, and Universal History / Susan Buck-Morss.
     p. cm. — (Illuminations : cultural formations of the Americas)
  Includes bibliographical references and index.
  ISBN-13: 978-0-8229-4340-2 (cloth : alk. paper)
  ISBN-10: 0-8229-4340-9 (cloth : alk. paper)
  ISBN-13: 978-0-8229-5978-6 (pbk. : alk. paper)
  ISBN-10: 0-8229-5978-X (pbk. : alk. paper)
  1. Hegel, Georg Wilhelm Friedrich, 1770–1831. 2. Haiti—History—
Revolution, 1791–1804. 3. Slavery. 4. History—Philosophy. I. Buck-Morss,
Susan. Universal history. II. Title. III. Title: Universal history.
  B2948.B845 2009
  193—dc22
                                2008048901

HEGEL, HAITI,

and Universal History

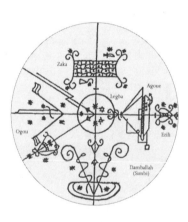

Illuminations: Cultural Formations of the Americas

John Beverley and Sara Castro-Klarén, Editors

CONTENTS

LIST OF ILLUSTRATIONS

Part One

Part Two

"HEGEL AND HAITI" was something of an intellectual event when it appeared in *Critical Inquiry* in the summer of 2000. The essay's unexpected movement through art catalogues, political journals, foreign translations, internet blogs, workers' newspapers, and college classrooms was in response to the unconventional topologies of time and space that it mapped out, perhaps more in tune with how we actually live our lives than the histories of separate pasts we have been taught. I am grateful for the interest and generosity of scholars, artists, and activists who found it useful in a variety of contexts, and from whom I have learned a great deal. The essay has generated controversy as well. It pleased the academic critics of Eurocentrism, but not entirely. While decentering the legacy of Western modernity (that was applauded), it proposed the less popular goal of salvaging modernity's universal intent, rather than calling for a plurality of alternative modernities. For some, the very suggestion of resurrecting the project of universal history from the ashes of modern metaphysics appeared tantamount to collusion with Western imperialism—or perhaps more precisely, American imperialism, a more abstract and some would say insidious form.

A second essay, "Universal History," appears here in response to the critics of the first. Far from recanting the earlier argument, it develops the most controversial claims. It writes history as political philosophy, assembling material related to "Hegel and Haiti" that changes what we think we know about the past, and therefore how we think the present. There is political urgency to this project.

The contemporary slogan, Think Global—Act Local, requires modification. We need first to ask what it means to Think Global, because we do not yet know how. We need to find ways through the *local* specificities of our own traditions toward a conceptual orientation that can inform *global* action. One way, developed in this volume, is to change the compass heading of particular historical data so that they point toward a universal history worthy of the name. There is no anticipation of unity in this task, no presumption that beneath the rhetoric of difference we are all unproblematically the same. Judgments of difference are not suspended. Political struggles continue. But they can take place without the traditional preconceptions that set barriers to moral imagination before deliberations even begin.

These essays are situated at the border between history and philosophy. The understanding of universal history they propose is distinct from Hegel's systematized comprehension of the past, just as it is from Heidegger's ontological claim that historicality is the essence of being. Universal history refers more to method than content. It is an orientation, a philosophical reflection grounded in concrete material, the conceptual ordering of which sheds light on the political present. The image of truth thereby revealed is time-sensitive. It is not that truth changes; we do.

If American history has anything to contribute to the project of universal humanity at *this* historical moment, it is the *idea* (of which reality has notoriously fallen short) that collective, political participation need not be based on custom or ethnicity, religion or race. American imperialism is hardly the origin of this idea. Far more, it is the experience of New World slavery. That is one of the conclusions of the second essay, "Universal History." Constructed out of historical fragments from multiple disciplines, it chips away at the barriers to conceptual understanding and the limits of moral imagination that wall off the wide horizon of the present. If this unapologetically humanist project, rather than quieting the critics of "Hegel and Haiti," raises the stakes of the controversy, it will have achieved its goal.

Thanks are due to my extraordinary graduate students and to my long-time colleagues in Cornell University's Government Department, especially Benedict Anderson, Martin Bernal, Mary Katzenstein, and Peter Katzenstein. Thanks to Hortense Spillers who supported the project's earliest stages, Iftikhar Dadi and Salah Hassan who brought "Hegel and Haiti" to the international attention of artists, Cynthia Chase who got the title right, Michael Kamnen who was there when I found *Minerva*, Teresa Brennan who gave me a room by the sea to work, and Zillah Eisenstein who has been with me every step of the way.

Thanks for his enthusiasm to W. J. T. Mitchell, editor of *Critical Inquiry*, the best journal of nondisciplined research published today. Thanks for debates and discussions of those invited to a Cornell conference on "Haiti and Universal History"—originally scheduled for September 2001 when no planes were flying, and held in November —both those who could come and those who could not: Jossianna Arroyo, Joan Dayan, Sibylle Fischer, J. Lorand Matory, Walter Mignolo, Marcus Rediker, and Michel-Rolph Trouillot. Thanks to Candido Mendes and the international community of scholars of the Académie de la Latinité who brought me and my work to Port-au-Prince, to Aurelio Alonso and Katherine Gordy who introduced "Hegel and Haiti" in Cuba, to Norma Publishers (Buenos Aires) for the Spanish translation, Éditions LIGNES (Paris) for the French, ombre corte (Verona) for the Italian, Haus der Kulturen der Welt (Berlin) for the German, Monikl (Istanbul) for the Turkish, and Seidosha (Tokyo) for the Japanese.

The participants of the Stone Summer Theory Institute at the School of the Art Institute of Chicago were the brilliantly spirited audience for the first public presentation of "Universal History" in 2007. Thanks to James Elkins for inviting me, and to Zhivka Valiavicharska, who was the first to name the method a New Humanism, resisting the monopoly of this term by the Right. Franz-Peter Hugdhal kindly read the page proof.

I am delighted to have this volume published in the series *Illuminations* edited by John Beverly and Sara Castro-Klarén, and grateful to Devin Fromm, Peter Kracht, and Alex Wolfe, editors of University of Pittsburgh Press, for their expertise and patient support.

Thanks finally to Eric Siggia and Sam Siggia, who give to daily existence solace and joy.

Hegel and Haiti

INTRODUCTION
TO PART ONE

First Remarks

"HEGEL AND HAITI" was written as a mystery story. The reader is encouraged to begin with it directly, before the introduction provided here. For those already familiar with the plot and its denouement, this new introduction (that can be read as the afterword as well) describes the process of discovery behind the essay and the impact of its first reception. It traces the years of research that led to "Hegel and Haiti," fleshing out material condensed in the footnotes so that the scholarly implications can be more easily ascertained, and situating the essay within ongoing intellectual debates that have real-world political implications.

The Accidental Project

I did not set out to write about Hegel or Haiti. In the 1990s, I was working on a different project. With the end of the Cold War, neoliberalism rose to ideological dominance on a global scale. Appeals to economic laws and market rationality were the legitimating mantra used to justify every kind of practical policy. Just what was this bodiless phantasm, "the economy," that was the object of such fetishistic reverence? When and why was it discovered, and more perplexing given its invisible hand, how? Adam Smith and the Scottish Enlightenment were the logical place to look, not just for the arguments of these philosophers but also for the context in which their ideas took hold.

Most surprising was how much intellectual excitement theories of political economy stirred up throughout Europe at the turn of the nineteenth century. By the time Marx studied economics two generations later, it was described as the "dismal science"; today's philosophers seldom show interest. Even if a few basic phrases have become staples of everyday thought (supply and demand; profit motive; competition), just how the economy works remains inscrutable to today's general public; it is knowledge reserved for a priesthood of experts who have inordinate power to determine our lives. No one reads economics journals for fun. So, what accounts for the enormous excitement with which the 1776 publication of Adam Smith's *Wealth of Nations* was received?

Hegel's early writings proved useful for this inquiry.[1] His Jena texts are a striking record of the impact of reading *Wealth of Nations* in 1803.[2] His philosophical attention was caught by Smith's description of the radically transforming effects of a deceptively simple innovation in manufacture: the division of labor. Using the mundane example of pin making, Smith argued that dividing production into

1. The results of this search into the origin of the economy, its mysterious invisibility, and Hegel's excited reception of Smith are discussed in Buck-Morss, "Envisioning Capital," 434–67. The idea that the economy has been an ahistorical constant since Aristotle is as erroneous as the claim that Aristotle was the source of Hegel's understanding of slavery.

2. Christian Garve produced an extremely good German translation (1784–96), but Hegel seems to have used the original English edition. Both versions, Smith's original and Garve's translation, were ultimately in Hegel's permanent library.

small, specialized tasks had an exponentially multiplying effect on both worker productivity and consumer need, hugely increasing the scope and degree of human interdependency.[3] Hegel was fascinated, perhaps terrified by the vision of limitless masses of pins being heaped upon the world, as well as the deadening effect that the repetitive, segmented actions of labor had upon the workers. He recognized that this new economy as a "system of need" had the power to alter the form of collective life.[4] His description was dramatic: "need and labor" create "a monstrous system of mutual dependency" that "moves about blindly, like the elements, and like a wild beast, requires steady and harsh taming and control."[5] By 1805–6, he was using the new economy in place of the traditional concept of "bourgeois" or "civil" society (*die bürgerliche Gesellschaft*) as

3. Hegel cites Smith's pin making example on multiple occasions—nearly every time making a new numerical mistake! Not the details of the new science intrigued him but, rather, Smith's innovative conceptualization (see Buck-Morss, "Envisioning Capital," 458n57). See Waszek, *Scottish Enlightenment,* for details on Hegel's reading of Adam Smith, including his poor mathematics regarding pin production, and indications that he was using Smith's original English text: "The recently discovered 1817/18 set of notes, taken by P. Wannenmann, is most interesting, because it documents the only time that Hegel reproduces Smith's calculation correctly" (*Scottish Enlightenment,* 131).

4. The term "system of need," referring to the satisfaction of need in general, first appears in Hegel, *System der Sittlichkeit* (1803), 80–84, and is cited from the 1967 edition, ed. Georg Lasson. "The satisfaction of needs is a general dependency of all upon each other" is his description in Fragment 22 of the 1803–4 manuscript that is referred to by Hoffmeister's standard edition of Hegel's works as *Jenenser Realphilosophie I,* and that is cited here from the more recent edition: Hegel, *Jenaer Systementwürfe I: Das System der spekulativen Philosophie,* eds. Klaus Düsing and Heinz Kimmerle (1986), 229 (323). This is the paperback, working version of volume 6 of the historical-critical edition of Hegel's *Gesammelten Werken;* I have added the pagination of volume 6 in parentheses as an aid to scholars.

I have made my own translations from the German. However, both of these Jena texts have been translated as Hegel, *System of Ethical Life (1802/3) and First Philosophy of Spirit (Part III of the System of Speculative Philosophy 1803/4),* ed. and trans. H. S. Harris and T. M. Knox (1979). This edition includes for the second text the pagination of volume 6 of the critical-historical edition, allowing the reader to compare my translation with theirs. For the 1802/3 text, my citations from the German include in parentheses the pagination of the 1923 edition of Georg Lasson (1913) that is noted in the Knox-Harris translation.

5. Hegel, *Jenaer Systementwürfe I,* 230 (324).

the basis of a philosophy of political constitutions that calls on the state to step forward as the force (*Gewalt*) of taming this wild and voracious animal.[6] His economic reworking of the concept of civil society has been described as "epoch-making."[7]

Bourgeois Society

Hegel was an acute observer of the rupture in social life that we now call modernity. The Jena lecture notes are full of its evidence. His lifelong project was to grasp this transformation in terms of its philosophical significance. Hegel's philosophical system may climb to abstract levels (a student who heard his early lectures at Jena claimed he "could make absolutely nothing of them, had no idea what was being discussed, ducks or geese"[8]), but his texts are full of the kind of historically concrete detail that theorists with a materialist bent like myself find particularly appealing: pin manufacturing, coffee drinking, poorhouses, men's frockcoats, corkscrews, and candlewick cutters. Even the most abstract terms of Hegel's con-

6. Hegel, *Jenaer Systementwürfe III*, 222–42 (242–65). This is the paperback, working version of volume 8 of the historical-critical edition (see note 4 above).

7. Riedel, *Between Tradition and Revolution*, 44. It was Christian Garve (A. Smith's translator) who observed the differentiation that had evolved in modern times within the term *die bürgerliche Gesellschaft* between the "citizen" (*citoyen*), a political concept within the traditional meaning of "civil society," and the "burger" (*bourgeois*), a nonpolitical, private person, the town-dwelling middle class (*Stand*) of traders and artisans, whose social relations are embedded in economic exchange. The increasing distinction in meaning, not registered in the English translation "civil society," has led to confusions. Hegel recognized the dual and, in his interpretation, dialectical unity of modern man as a public and a private person in *Jenaer Systementwürfe III*, 238 (261). For an excellent essay that traces these complications, see Riedel, *"Bürger,"* 672–725.

8. Cited in Petry, *Hegel's Philosophy of Subjective Spirit*, 1:xvi. The situation did not improve with Hegel's advancing career. Petry cites a young Estonian nobleman who, when he arrived at the University of Heidelberg in 1817, went "to the first good bookshop, bought those of Hegel's works available, and that evening settled comfortably on the sofa, intending to read them through . . . But the more I read, the more strenuously I applied myself to what I was reading, the less I understood, and after I had struggled in vain for a couple of hours with one of the sentences, I was quite out of temper, and put the book aside. Out of curiosity, I later attended the lectures, but I must confess that I was unable to understand the notes I had taken" (*Hegel's Philosophy of Subjective Spirit*, 1:xvi).

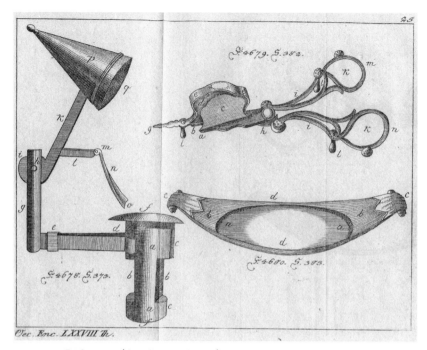

FIGURE I. Lichtputze (Candlewick Cutter).

ceptual vocabulary are derived from everyday experience. In the Jena writings, the central Hegelian term "objectification" (*Entäusserung*) has, as its referent, mundane human labor; "negation" is Hegelian for the desire of consumption; and historically created needs, as opposed to natural necessity, are exemplified in the social imitation of fashion.

The system of need is the social connection among strangers who neither know nor care about each other. The "insatiable desire" of consumers, combined with the "inexhaustible and illimitable production" of "what the English call 'comfort,'" produces "the movement of things" that has no discernable limits.[9] Hegel is in fact

9. Cited in Waszek, *Scottish Enlightenment*, 150, 152, and Hegel, *Jenaer Systementwürfe III*, 208 (227); it is the interdependency of the division of labor that gives desire "the right to appear" (*Jenaer Systementwürfe III*, 208 [227]).

describing the deterritoralized, world market of the European colonial system, and he is the first philosopher to do so.[10] This accidental, blind dependency no longer refers, as in the tradition of civic humanism, to the contractual relationships among property holders as public citizens that provide the basis for shared consent to the laws of government. It is society created by political economy as Adam Smith conceived it—still urban or "bourgeois" (*bürgerliche*) society, to be sure, but transformed by the modern realities of colonial trade. The new merchant class (*Handelsstand*) is comprised of long-distance traders. Their interest is less (as Hobbes understood) to secure their property, than to secure the terms of its "alienation" (*Entfremdung*), their right to buy and sell. Hegel recognizes that whereas the things exchanged are equal in value, the paradoxical social consequence is *in*equality, "the antithesis of great wealth and great poverty": "to him who has, more is given."[11] Commercial exchange creates a continually self-reproducing network of relations between persons—"'society' in the modern sense of the word."[12]

The new society is not an ethnic group or kin-based clan (*Stamm*). It is the dissolution of the *Volk* as traditionally conceived.[13] Compared

10. Hegel's understanding of the role of colonies in producing this "system of need" (*System der Sittlichkeit*, 77–80 [485–88]), the instabilities caused by consumer dependency on products from "abroad" (*System der Sittlichkeit*, 83 [491]), as well as the dehumanizing, exploitation of labor that undergirds competitive, global trade, distinguishes his discussion from the benign anticipation, more common among Enlightenment philosophers, that increasing commerce would bring about international peace and mutual understanding. While Kant and others had a strong *moral* criticism of the "injustices" of colonialism, this does not amount to a philosophical comprehension of the new society. See Muthu, *Enlightenment Against Empire*, for an informed and sympathetic discussion of Kant, Diderot, and Herder (that appears unaware, hence unwarrantedly dismissive of Hegel).

11. Hegel, *Jenaer Systementwürfe III*, 223 (244); see also Buck-Morss, "Envisioning Capital," 458. The remarkable degree to which Hegel's understanding of bourgeois society in these early writings dovetails with that of Marx is the theme of Marcuse, *Reason and Revolution*; and Lukács, *Der junge Hegel*.

12. Riedel, *Between Tradition and Revolution*, 45.

13. "The absolute bond of the people, namely the ethical (*das Sittliche*), has vanished, and the people (*Volk*) is dissolved" (Hegel, *System der Sittlichkeit*, 84.) The new society produces a different form of ethics. *Sittlichkeit* is translated as "ethical life," but it

with civil society in the old sense, bourgeois society is unpatriotic, driven to push beyond national limits in trade. Commerce is borderless; its place is the sea. Strictly speaking, the economy and the nation are incompatible (Smith saw the colonial economy as distorting the national polity[14]). The economy is infinitely expansive; the nation constrains and sets bounds. Hegel ultimately resolves this opposition between the force of society and the force of the state, which produces the Janus-faced individual as *bourgeois/citoyen*, by the introduction of a political constitution as a different form of interdependency, providing an ethical corrective to social inequalities through laws so that each aspect, civil society and the state, enables the other through their mutual opposition.[15]

In his reading of Adam Smith, Hegel saw a description of society that challenged the British and French enlightenment tradition on its most sacred ground: the state of nature. Far from a historical invariant and in stark opposition to natural law theory, this is a historically specific anthropology of mutual dependency. Whereas contract theory from Hobbes, to Locke, to Rousseau posited the independent and free individual possessed of natural liberties as the starting point of philosophical speculation, determining the

---

is not misleading for us to understand it in terms of "culture" in its anthropological senses (whereas the Hegelian word *Bildung*, translated as "culture," means educated or "cultivated"). The new *Sittlichkeit* refers to the culture, not of an ethnic people, but of a social form. Hegel believes, for example, that *Bildung* has become the new ethos in modern society: the education of individuals to reason, or self-consciousness, replaces the form of ethical life based in the family, which is collective, customary, and largely unreflected. It is this understanding of *Sittlichkeit*, I am arguing, that allows him to imagine African-born slaves adopting the self-conscious ethos of modern political life.

14. This is a constant theme in his writings. Merchant capital is, for example, inherently unpatriotic: "A merchant, it has been said very properly, is not necessarily the citizen of any particular country" (Smith, *The Wealth of Nations*, 519).

15. This theme, anticipated in the final section, "Constitution," of Hegel, *Jenaer Systementwürfe III*, 238 (261) (see also above, note 7), is elaborated in the *Philosophy of Right* (1821). Many themes from the Jena lectures reappear in lectures on the philosophy of right that Hegel gave almost yearly from 1817/18 to 1825/26 (student notes taken from these have survived).

terms for entering into societal and contractual agreements, Hegel's modern subject is *already* in a web of social dependencies because of commodity exchange. But how does Hegel move from the economy to the state? Riedel observes only that the state appears as a deus ex machina to rescue the new society from limitlessness and assert control.[16] And here is where things get interesting.

"Robinson Crusoe and Friday"[17]

As Hegel is describing the new society in the various Jena lectures, exploring the theme of "mutual recognition" as "recognition through exchange" (*Anerkanntsein im Tausch*), he speaks for the first time of the relationship between "master" and "slave."[18] The reader cannot help but be struck by the fact that this theme pops up alongside the description of the system of need in all of the texts. We are compelled to ask: what is the connection between the master-slave relationship and the new global economy? What, following the experts, would lead us to believe that he is appealing here to Aristotle? And if he is using slavery allegorically to describe only the domestic side of the French Revolution, then what does that have to do with the simultaneous discussion of commodity trade?

In the 1805–6 Jena texts, Hegel moves in rapid succession among economic themes (pin making, the movement of things in exchange, the dehumanization of the worker) and the political themes of master and slave and the "struggle of life and death," wherein "mutual recognition" appears "in its extreme form" (adding the marginal notation: "violence, domination and submission").[19] Conceptually, the revolutionary struggle of slaves, who overthrow

16. Riedel, *Between Tradition and Revolution*, 125.
17. See "Hegel and Haiti," 6In114.
18. The details of these are spelled out in the text and footnotes of "Hegel and Haiti," section 8, beginning on page 52.
19. Hegel, *Jenaer Systementwürfe III*, 203 (222).

FIGURE 2. Frontispiece to the 1785 edition of Daniel Defoe's 1719 novel, *Robinson Crusoe*, vol. 1. Illustrated by Mather Brown, engraved by Robert Pollard. From Blewett, *Illustrations of Robinson Crusoe*.

their own servitude and establish a constitutional state, provides the theoretical hinge that takes Hegel's analysis out of the limitlessly expanding colonial economy and onto the plane of world history, which he defines as the realization of freedom—a theoretical solution that was taking place in practice in Haiti at that very moment. The connection seems obvious, so obvious that the burden of proof would seem to fall on those who wish to argue otherwise. The interpretation supports Ritter's generally accepted thesis that with Hegel, "philosophy becomes the theory of its age,"[20] and it eliminates what bothered Riedel, the apparent arbitrariness of introducing the state as a deus ex machina. Mutual recognition among equals emerges with logical necessity out of the contradictions of slavery, not the least of which is trading human slaves as, legally, "things," when they show themselves capable of becoming the active agents of history by struggling against slavery in a "battle of recognition" under the banner, "Liberty or Death!"[21] What, then, would account for two centuries of historical oblivion?

This is the puzzle that launched the writing of "Hegel and Haiti." It led in unexpected directions, tugging me into a whole web of related evidence that shifted the focus toward Haiti, to be sure, but even more toward the issue of scholarship, and how the construction of an object of research over time can hide as much as it illuminates. Ultimately, "Hegel and Haiti" is about the connection, the "and" that links these two historical phenomena in silence. What drove me, and in fact angered me in the course of this research was an increasing awareness of the limits that scholarship places upon our imagination, so that the phenomenon called Hegel and the phenomenon called Haiti, porously interconnected at the time of their

20. "Just as the people had raised it as their banner, so Hegel takes up the idea of freedom and makes it the 'basic element' and 'sole matter' of his philosophy....Hegel in this way makes philosophy the theory of the age" (Ritter, *Hegel and the French Revolution*, 48).

21. Riedel, *Between Tradition and Revolution*, 125. See also "Hegel and Haiti," 54n93.

origins (as newspapers and journals clearly document) had become severed by the history of their transmission. To evoke the specter of Eurocentrism at this point is easy, of course, but it begs the question of how Eurocentrism itself was constructed historically, and what role Haiti might have played in that process.

Shifts in historical interpretation are not the invention of one person. The work of unrelated scholars builds upon each other. The Hegel scholars have been meticulous in their documentation, and precisely because of their thoroughness, it is possible to locate the holes in our knowledge that more careless research would have obscured. These holes reveal the fragments of another story behind the official one, and in trying to put parts of it together, I discovered writers from diverse disciplines whose scholarship is some of the most exciting and original of our time. The Haitian Revolution lies at the crossroads of multiple discourses as a defining moment in world history. It is impossible to swallow Samuel Huntington's glib dismissal of Haiti as fully marginal to the history of civilizations, a "lone country" that "lacks cultural commonality with other societies,"[22] after reading Joan Dayan, *Haiti, History and the Gods*, Sibylle Fischer, *Modernity Disavowed*, Peter Linebaugh and Marcus Rediker, *The Many-Headed Hydra*, Michel-Rolf Trouillot, *Silencing the Past*, and the many essays by David P. Geggus, not to speak of the classics: C.L.R. James, *The Black Jacobins* (1938), Eric Williams, *Capitalism and Slavery* (1944), David Brion Davis, *The Problem of Slavery in the Age of Revolution* (1975), Robin Blackburn, *The Overthrow of Colonial Slavery* (1988), and Paul Gilroy, *The Black Atlantic* (1992).

"Hegel and Haiti" supports a shift in knowledge away from traditional hierarchies of significance. It insists that facts are important not as data with fixed meanings, but as connective pathways that can continue to surprise us. Facts should inspire imagination

22. Huntington, *Clash of Civilizations*, 136.

rather than tying it down. The less they are subsumed under the fiction of secure knowledge, marshaled as proof of a predetermined and authoritative thesis, the more truth they are capable of revealing. Instead of defending a notion of intellectual turf, the point of scholarly debate should be to extend the horizon of historical imagination. There is a politics to such collective scholarship. Its goal is to produce knowledge for a global public sphere worthy of the name, where defining boundaries are not determined in advance as a consequence of monopoly control over knowledge by history's winners.

Hegel knew, but does it matter?

For raising the question of whether Hegel was indeed inspired by events in Saint-Domingue, credit must go to Pierre-Franklin Tavarès. Drawing on French, rather than German sources and relying on his own sound intuitions, Tavarès wrote a series of brief, speculative articles in the early 1990s that made bold claims: Hegel was "preoccupied" from the earliest years with the contemporary issue of slavery; criticisms of slavery can be detected even when camouflaged in the garb of the ancients; the young Hegel, reader of the Abbé Raynal's history of the Indies, was better informed about Caribbean slavery than he let it appear; indeed, Hegel remained a "Raynalist" throughout his life.[23]

Since the publication of "Hegel and Haiti," Nick Nesbitt has initiated a reading of Hegel's mature work, the *Philosophy of Right* (1821), from the perspective of the Saint-Domingue slaves, con-

23. Thanks to Pierre-Franklin Tavarès, and to Henry Robert Jolibois of the Haitian Ministry of Culture, for making available to me these articles, that grew out of Tavarès' work on a doctoral dissertation (Tavarès, "Hegel, critique de l'Afrique"). See "La Conception de l'Afrique de Hegel," 153–66; "Hegel et l'abbé Grégoire," 155–73; "Hegel et Haïti," 113–31; "Hegel, philosophe anti-esclavagiste." Tavarès currently writes on the contemporary crisis in the Ivory Coast, as official in charge of Franco-African affairs in the office of the Mayor of Epinay-sur-Seine.

cluding that this "progressive" text moves further than the abstractions of the more "timid" *Phenomenology*, providing "the first great analysis of the Haitian Revolution" in its "explication and radical defense of the right of slaves to revolt."[24] While we may differ in our emphasis and disagree on details, Tavarès and Nesbitt, focusing on different texts, concur as to the obviousness of the connection.[25] As far as Haitian scholars are concerned, they were not surprised by my presentation of "Hegel and Haiti" in Port-au-Prince in 2005 (they already knew of Tavarès's articles).[26]

It is curious that Tavarès's speculations have not been more widely debated, and I regret having come upon his articles so late in my own research. But before rushing too quickly to see this scholar, an African, as victim of Euro-American academic hegemony (Tavarès, a French citizen, studied in Paris; the Hegel establishment has shown no great interest in my own work), we need to consider not only Hegel's Haiti, but Haiti's Hegel, that is, the Afro-Caribbean reception of Hegel that claims him as their own. Nesbitt has traced this legacy through the work of Aimé Césaire, whose influential conception of *negritude*, referring to the African diaspora's self-understanding based on "a common experience of subjugation and enslavement," considers the slave's self-liberation in the Haitian Revolution as "emblematic."[27] Césaire recalled to Nesbitt personally his youthful excitement in discovering Hyppolite's new translation

24. Nesbitt, "Troping Toussaint, Reading Revolution," 18–33.

25. Nesbitt has the most radical reading of Hegel. Tavarès' reading, through the French sources, tones down Hegel's politics, suggesting that Hegel was always a gradualist, believing that slaves through the discipline of work earned their freedom, whereas the too rapid liberation of the slaves declared by Toussaint marked their "second defeat" (Tavarès, "Hegel, philosophe anti-esclavagiste," 27).

26. *Chemins Critiques*, the journal in which several of Tavarès' articles appeared, is a Haitian publication. Thanks to Marie-Lucie Vendryes, director general of the Musée Pantheon National Haitien, Republic of Haiti, for her comments on my presentation.

27. Cited in Nesbitt, *Voicing Memory*, 21. Nesbitt discusses Hegel's *Phenomenology* with Césaire's 1963 play *La Tragédie du roi Christophe*, as putting together Yoruba/Vodou and Hegelian philosophies of history (*Voicing Memory*, 143).

of Hegel's *Phenomenology* (1941): "When the French translation of the *Phenomenology* first came out, I showed it to Senghor, and said to him 'Listen to what Hegel says, Léopold: to arrive at the Universal, one must immerse oneself in the Particular!'"[28] Césaire understood that the truly productive, "universal" experience of reading Hegel is not through a summary of the total and totalizing system, but through the liberation that one's own imagination can achieve by encountering dialectical thinking in its most concrete exemplification.

If the question of Hegel's sources were all that was at stake, the results might be incorporated into present disciplinary structures, contested or not among Hegel scholars as a source of influence or explanation of context, but not essential to the meaning of the famous dialectic of master and slave. The history of philosophic scholarship is an example of how the colonial experience has been excluded from the stories Western thought tells about itself. As a certain professor of philosophy told me frankly, "even if Hegel were writing with Haiti in mind, it would not change the way that I teach Hegel"—a remarkable statement that from a certain perspective is justified, of course, but it was precisely this perspective that I was hoping to unsettle, placing emphasis on the linking conjunction, the "and," to the point where we cannot think Hegel *without* Haiti. Scholars of modern philosophies of freedom are hobbled in attempting to do their work in ignorance of Haitian history. Historical context permeates modern philosophy—that was indeed Hegel's modernist, self-conscious intent. But the reverse is true as well. Because of his own insistence on the necessary interconnection between history and truth, Hegel's philosophy cannot be divorced from the repressions through which the referent that we call Hegel has come to be historically known.

28. Nesbitt, *Voicing Memory*, 120.

Hegel's Silence

One caveat deserves consideration. If it is indisputable that Hegel knew about Haiti, as did indeed the entire European reading public, why is there not more explicit discussion in his texts? Nesbitt considers the references direct enough for anyone living at the time to understand, and that may be. But the fact that they have been systematically overlooked for several centuries is not only the responsibility of later scholars. To what degree is Hegel himself accountable for the effective silencing of the Haitian Revolution? Tavarès speaks specifically to this point, claiming that *le silence de Hegel* is a consequence of his connections with Freemasonry. Drawing from the work of Jacques d'Hondt, he argues that Hegel's tendency to "dissimulate or keep silent regarding certain of his sources of documentation and information" was typical of members of the secret brotherhood, which particularly in these revolutionary times was under political suspicion.[29] D'Hondt insists that this connection makes an esoteric reading of Hegel necessary generally.[30]

Without doubt, the influence of Freemasonry was profound at the time, fusing contradictory desires for political secrecy and public transparency, enlightenment reason and hermetic mysticism, modernism and eternal knowledge. Freemasonry is a continuous thread in the story of Hegel and Haiti, connecting the slave-trading ports of Bordeaux, the plantations of Saint-Domingue, English antislavery authors, the journalists reporting for *Minerva* from Paris, and book publishers in Germany.[31] Hegel was part of this vast, communicating network, which he knew to include Garve, Archenholz,

29. Tavarès, "Hegel et Haïti," 119.

30. See d'Hondt, *Hegel Secret*, especially chap. 1, "Minerva," which deals with the journal's coverage of the French Revolution (but not its frequent articles on Saint-Domingue; hence Tavarès's omission of this connection). On d'Hondt, see "Hegel and Haiti," 62n121.

31. See "Hegel and Haiti," section 10, beginning on page 60.

Rainsford, Cotta, and Oelsner (all of whom make an appearance in "Hegel and Haiti"). One cannot help but be struck by the affinities between the politics of Hegel's early philosophy of spirit, and his reading of the journal *Minerva*, with its Mason-spirited endorsement of Girondin cosmopolitanism committed to the international spread of revolutionary ideals, explicitly including Toussaint L'Overture's republic, yet critical of what Hegel in the *Phenomenology* called the "abstract negation" of revolutionary terror.

Oelsner's Historical Letters from Paris, published in *Minerva*, criticized the local Jacobins as "cannibals" (*Menschenfleischfresser*). He deplored their striving for "a wild democracy" that could drive "the most civilized nation into the deepest barbarism."[32] And it was Rainsford, also part of the *Minerva* Freemasonry network, who made the contrary historical movement explicit: while the "assassins and executioners" of Jacobin France were causing "a great and polished nation" to return to "the barbarism of the earliest periods," the world saw in the "Black Republic," the rise of "negroes emancipating themselves from the vilest slavery, and at once filling the relations of society, enacting laws, and commanding armies, leaving slavery's barbarism behind."[33] (These cosmopolitans were not guilty of the later charge that Europeans failed to recognize the barbarism of their own modernity.[34])

32. Cited in Saine, *Black Bread–White Bread*, 292. There were many such comparisons to barbarism and cannibalism at the time, documented by Saine, who gives repeated evidence that the masses were not included in German liberal affirmations of the revolutionary French Republic. *Volk* is simply not a positive category in eighteenth-century German thought. While not mentioning Hegel as one of the readers of *Minerva*, Saine underlines the importance of this journal, and specifically the reports by Oelsner (whom we know Hegel met in Berne): "One must in fact seriously weigh the possibility that it was the lengthy and detailed dispatches by Oelsner and the young 'Freiheitssoldat' (an anonymous soldier for freedom) in the *Minerva*—without a doubt the most influential and widely read journal dealing with contemporary affairs—which more than anything else influenced the German liberals' view of the revolution at this stage [August 1792]" (*Black Bread–White Bread*, 361).

33. Rainsford, *Historical Account*, x–xi. Rainsford is making the contrast too strong, as Haiti clearly had its own Revolutionary Terror.

34. See the discussion of this charge in Fischer, *Modernity Disavowed*.

Sibylle Fischer is right to observe that by breaking off his dis-
cussion of the master-slave dialectic *before* the slave rebels, Hegel
invites readers of the *Phenomenology* (including his own contempo-
raries) to "fill in the sketchy transition," and that this invitation has
led over the years to "some of the most profound disagreements in
the Hegel literature."[35] Silence has the power of eliciting conjec-
ture, and as the figure is Hegel, whose authority is beyond question,
we are quick to presume an authorial reason for this silence.[36] Yet
the simplest answer may be the most adequate.

In the Jena years, Hegel was feeling anything but the great figure
we now take him to be. When he completed the *Phenomenology*, he was
only thirty-six, and his life was in shambles. Terry Pinkard's recent
biography describes Hegel's existential destitution: "With no money,
no real paying job, and a child by a woman who was married to
someone who had recently abandoned her [Hegel's landlord!],
Hegel's situation now became completely and totally desperate."[37]
Such a man was not likely to include in his first major publication
explicit references to Haiti that would be appreciated by neither the

35. Fischer, *Modernity Disavowed*, 28. As a contrast to my own interpretation of
Hegel as an admirer of the slave revolution, she refers to Judith Butler's inquiry into
this silence, that concludes Hegel's resolution of the dialectic was "dystopic," analogous
to Foucault's view, "according to which subjects cannot, in the strict sense, be liberated
from oppression, since they come into existence only as effects of just that oppression"
(*Modernity Disavowed*, 28). Butler is not arguing for historical intent; her textual inter-
pretation is consciously mediated by the present—as is mine from a different critical-
theoretical perspective. While differing in method, as far as the politics of our work is
concerned, Butler and I are not as opposed in our "ideological commitments" (*Modernity
Disavowed*, 28) as it might appear.
    36. Fischer interprets Hegel's silence psychoanalytically: "This, it strikes me, is
the story of 'Hegel and Haiti.' It is a story of deep ambivalence, probably fascination,
probably fear, and ultimately disavowal" (*Modernity Disavowed*, 32).
    37. Pinkard, *Hegel*, 230. "In 1806, Goethe finally managed to get Hegel a salary
of 100 Thalers [an amount made famous by Kant's example in *The Critique of Pure Reason!*],
but this "amounted to little more than an honorarium" (*Hegel*, 223). Hegel, after at-
taining bourgeois respectability through an acceptable marriage, ultimately took finan-
cial responsibility for his illegitimate son, Ludwig, whom he encouraged when a young
man to join the Dutch merchant marines. Ludwig died in southeast Asia in 1831, the
same year as Hegel.

present German authorities, nor Napoleon who was responsible for Toussaint L'Overture's recent death and was just then invading Hegel's city. The aspiring philosopher, who was staking out as his life's work the task of grasping in philosophy the historical events of the age, was not about to get himself arrested.[38]

French soldiers in Jena ransacked the house where Hegel was staying: "Knaves have, to be sure, messed up my papers like lottery tickets."[39] To leave Jena, he seized the only job opportunity his friends could find him, and moved to Bamberg to edit a daily political newspaper, the *Bamberger Zeitung,* that was sympathetic to Napoleon in its outlook.[40] There are thus multiple, quite mundane reasons for Hegel's silence, from fear of political repercussions, to the impact of Napoleon's victory, to the hazards of moving and personal uprootings. There is cause to wonder about the fate of missing evidence—the "mere history" that was discarded from the end of the 1803 *System der Sittlichkeit;*[41] the last page(s) of the final fragment 22 that are missing from the 1803–4 Jena System[42]—as well as the motives of Hegel's posthumous editors in making the official selection of his works.[43] But there is no doubt that Hegel and Haiti belong together.

38. He was dazzled to see Napoleon—"this world-soul"—who rode into Jena the day before the battle (October 1806): "It is indeed a wonderful sensation to see such an individual, who, concentrated here at a single point, astride a horse, reaches out over the world and masters it . . . this extraordinary man, whom it is impossible not to admire" (Hegel's letter to Niethammer, cited in Pinkard, *Hegel,* 228). But as Pinkard notes, it is mythical to make too much of this now legendary meeting, as the *Phenomenology* had already been written, and as Hegel also experienced the horrors of the battle: "nobody has imagined war as we have seen it" (cited in Pinkard, *Hegel,* 230)

39. Cited in Pinkard, *Hegel,* 228.

40. Pinkard, *Hegel,* 242–43. Hegel wrote in positive anticipation, "I pursue world events with curiosity"; he hoped to bring the newspaper to the level of the French press, while maintaining the "pedantry and impartiality in news reports that above all the Germans demand."

41. According to its early editor (Rudolf Haym) the lecture manuscript from which this text was published (in 1857), degenerated into "mere history," and it is at least conceivable that this history, ignored by Haym, bore on events in Saint-Domingue. See "Hegel and Haiti," 53n91.

42. See "Hegel and Haiti," 52n90.

43. See "Hegel and Haiti," 49n82.

HEGEL AND HAITI*

1

BY THE EIGHTEENTH CENTURY, slavery had become the root metaphor of Western political philosophy, connoting everything that was evil about power relations.[1] Freedom, its conceptual antithesis, was considered by Enlightenment thinkers as the highest and universal political value. Yet this political metaphor began to take root at precisely the time that the economic practice of slavery—the systematic, highly sophisticated capitalist enslavement of non-Europeans as a labor force in the colonies—was increasing quantitatively and intensifying qualitatively to the point that by the mid-eighteenth century it came to underwrite the entire economic system of the West, paradoxically facilitating the global spread of the very Enlightenment ideals that were in such fundamental contradiction to it.

*This chapter was previously published as "Hegel and Haiti" in *Critical Inquiry* 26 (Summer 2000): 821–65. It is reprinted here with only minor changes.

1. "For eighteenth-century thinkers who contemplated the subject, slavery stood as the central metaphor for all the forces that debased the human spirit" Davis, *Problem of Slavery in the Age of Revolution*, 263.

This glaring discrepancy between thought and practice marked the period of the transformation of global capitalism from its mercantile to its protoindustrial form. One would think that, surely, no rational, "enlightened" thinker could have failed to notice. But such was not the case.

The exploitation of millions of colonial slave laborers was accepted as part of the given world by the very thinkers who proclaimed freedom to be man's natural state and inalienable right. Even when theoretical claims of freedom were transformed into revolutionary action on the political stage, it was possible for the slave-driven colonial economy that functioned behind the scenes to be kept in darkness.

If this paradox did not seem to trouble the logical consciousness of contemporaries, it is perhaps more surprising that present-day writers, while fully cognizant of the facts, are still capable of constructing Western histories as coherent narratives of human freedom. The reasons do not need to be intentional. When national histories are conceived as self-contained, or when the separate aspects of history are treated in disciplinary isolation, counterevidence is pushed to the margins as irrelevant. The greater the specialization of knowledge, the more advanced the level of research, the longer and more venerable the scholarly tradition, the easier it is to ignore discordant facts. It should be noted that specialization and isolation are also a danger for those new disciplines such as African American studies, or new fields such as diaspora studies, that were established precisely to remedy the situation. Disciplinary boundaries allow counterevidence to belong to someone else's story. After all, a scholar cannot be an expert in everything. Reasonable enough. But such arguments are a way of avoiding the awkward truth that if certain constellations of facts are able to enter scholarly consciousness deeply enough, they threaten not only the venerable narratives, but also the entrenched academic disciplines that (re)produce them. For example, there is no place in the university in which the particular research constellation "Hegel and Haiti" would have a home. That is the topic which concerns me here, and I am going to take a circuitous route to reach it. My apologies, but this apparent detour is the argument itself.

2

The paradox between the discourse of freedom and the practice of slavery marked the ascendancy of a succession of Western nations within the early modern global economy. The earliest example to consider would be the Dutch. Their "Golden Age," from the mid-sixteenth to the mid-seventeenth century, was made possible by their dominance of global mercantile trade, including, as a fundamental component the trade in slaves. But if we follow its most excellent of modern historians, Simon Schama, whose thick description of the Golden Age of Dutch culture has become a model in the field of cultural history since its publication in 1987, we will be in for a surprise. Strikingly, the topics of slavery, the slave trade, and slave labor are never discussed in Schama's *The Embarrassment of Riches*, a six hundred-plus-page account of how the new Dutch Republic, in developing its own national culture, learned to be both rich and good.[2] One would have no idea that Dutch hegemony in the slave trade (replacing Spain and Portugal as major players)[3]

2. See Schama, *Embarrassment of Riches*. The question for this newly enriched nation was "how to create a moral order *within* a terrestrial paradise" (*Embarrassment of Riches*, 125).

3. The Spanish *asiento* granted to individuals the exclusive privilege of providing Spanish America with African slaves, but the Spanish themselves only loosely controlled the trade. Slave trading posts on the African coast flew flags of Portugal, Holland, France, England, Denmark, and Brandenburg as well. The Dutch merchant marines dominated shipping among the North Sea countries, carrying the goods of other nations, and they were participants in the *asiento* slave trade as well.

contributed substantially to the enormous "overload" of wealth that he describes as becoming so socially and morally problematic during the century of Dutch "centrality" to the "commerce of the world."[4] Yet Schama reports fully the fact that the metaphor of slavery, adapted to the modern context from the Old Testament story of the Israelites' deliverance from Egyptian slavery was fundamental to Dutch self-understanding during their struggle for independence (1570–1609) against the Spanish "tyranny" that "enslaved" them—and hence for the origins of the modern Dutch nation.[5] Schama clearly acknowledges the most blatant contradiction, the fact that the Dutch discriminated at the time against Jews.[6] He includes a whole chapter discussing the scapegoating and persecution of a long list of "outsiders" who, due to the Dutch psychological obsession for purification, needed to be cleansed from the social body: homosexuals, Jews, gypsies, idlers, vagabonds, whores—but has nothing to say about African slaves in this context.[7]

4. Schama, *Embarrassment of Riches*, 228. My reading revealed only two mentions of real slavery: in a discussion of the Dutch feasting habits, a distaste for *"mengelmoes* (mishmash)," which was a "soupy pabulum," "the pap of slaves and babies" (*Embarrassment of Riches*, 177), and mention that the Dutch West India Company was "forced to spend well over a million guilders a year in defending the footholds at Recife and Pernambuco [in Brazil against the Portuguese], while only four hundred thousand guilders in profits had been made off the receipts from slaving and the sugar and dyewood plantations it supplied" (*Embarrassment of Riches*, 252).

5. The "Exodus epic became for the Dutch what it had been for the Biblical Jews: the legitimation of a great historical rupture, a cut with the past which had made possible the retrospective invention of a collective identity" (Schama, *Embarrassment of Riches*, 113). King Philip XI of Spain was likened to the Pharaoh during the Egyptian enslavement: "*'The one bowed down Jacob's house* [Israelites] *with slavery / The other, the Netherlands oppressed with tyranny'*" (105). The Dutch reference to the Catholic missionary Bartolomé de Las Casas's biting condemnation of the Spanish "misdeeds" of slavery in the colonies is mentioned by Schama, even as the Dutch practice of slavery is not (*Embarrassment of Riches*, 84).

6. "Paradoxically, the church's predilection for describing its own flock as the reborn Hebrews did not dispose it to favor the real thing" (Schama, *Embarrassment of Riches*, 591).

7. See Schama, *Embarrassment of Riches*, 565–608. Schama describes connections made by the Dutch between non-Europeans and excesses of tobacco, sexuality, and other debaucheries that threatened to contaminate the Dutch domestically: "The stock

Schama is clearly fatigued with the Marxist economic histories that treat the Dutch *only* as a mercantile capitalist power.[8] His project is, rather, the tracing of cultural causality. He examines how the anxieties of affluence due to the "overflow of goods" awakened in the modern Dutch the fear of a different kind of slavery, the "enslavement to luxury" that threatened "free will," the fear that avarice to consume would "turn free souls into fawning slaves."[9] He focuses on the family as the core of "Dutchness," not world trade, allowing his readers entry into private, domestic life, home and hearth, full tables and personal affections, when "to *be* Dutch was to be local, parochial, traditional and customary."[10] We might be ready, therefore, to excuse him—were it not for the fact that slaves were not foreign to Dutch domesticity. Does Schama's silence reflect the silence of his written sources? I cannot tell.[11] But Dutch visual culture provides clear evidence of a different reality. A painting by Franz Hals from 1648 depicts at the very center of the canvas a black youth, presumably a slave, as part of domestic life, visible in the bosom of

---

visual and textual anthologies of native barbarism in Brazil and Florida, for example, featured Indians smoking through rolled leaves, while acts of copulation, cannibalism, public urination and other sorts of miscellaneous beastliness proceeded routinely in the background" (*Embarrassment of Riches*, 204).

8. Schama is happy simply to record without critical comment the magical fantasy of Thomas Mun, that under capitalism money begets money, as influencing the Dutch he is studying: "Capital begot capital with astonishing ease, and so far from denying themselves its fruits, capitalists reveled in the material comforts it bought. At midcentury there seemed no limit, certainly no geographical limit, to the range of its fleets and the resourcefulness of its entrepreneurs. No sooner was one consumer demand glutted or exhausted than another promising raw material was discovered, the supply monopolized, demand stimulated, markets exploited at home and abroad. Would the tide of prosperity ever ebb?" (*Embarrassment of Riches*, 323).

9. Schama, *Embarrassment of Riches*, 47, 203.

10. Schama, *Embarrassment of Riches*, 62.

11. Certainly Grotius discussed real slavery. But Grotius (see below, note 15) is cited by Schama only in other contexts (just wars, free trade, Dutch destiny, marriage, whales). It is not unreasonable to have suspicions that the silence is Schama's own. Such selective national histories have become a trend in European historiography, one that omits much or all of the colonizing story.

a comfortable, affectionate Dutch family within a local, parochial, Dutch landscape. In Schama's richly illustrated book, this painting by Hals does not appear (although another Hals painting, of a Dutch husband and wife alone in a landscape, is included). Nor are there any other images of blacks.[12] Of course, given the absence of slaves from Schama's written account, they would have been out of place in the illustrations. The consequence of this scholarship is partial blindness among seas of perspicacity, and it is characteristic of Western academic scholarship, as we shall see.

3

Beginning in 1651, Britain challenged the Dutch in a series of naval wars that led ultimately to British dominance not only of Europe but of the global economy, including the slave trade.[13] At the time, the Cromwellian revolution against absolute monarchy and feudal privilege followed Dutch precedent by making metaphorical use of the Old Testament story of the Israelites being freed from slavery. But within political theory a shedding of ancient scriptures was taking place. The pivotal figure here is Thomas Hobbes. Although *Leviathan* (1651) is a hybrid of modern and biblical imagery, slavery is discussed in clearly secular terms.[14] He sees it as a consequence of the war of all against all in the state of nature, hence belonging

12. Although see Blakeley, *Blacks in the Dutch World*, which gives visual evidence of blacks in Holland in this era.

13. Britain extorted the *asiento* from Spain at the time of the Treaty of Utrecht (1713). "Much of the wealth of Bristol and Liverpool in the following decades was to be built upon the slave trade" (Palmer and Colton, *History of the Modern World*, 171).

14. If Hobbes's rhetorical examples draw on machinery as a metaphor for the artificially constructed state, the Old Testament provides the title for *Leviathan*, as it does for Hobbes's book on the Long Parliament, *Behemoth*, the biblical name for a tyrannical sovereign, already in use in the Dutch national story: "The kings of Spain in whose name these infamies [against Dutch civilian populations] . . . came to be seen as Behemoth, determined on destroying the bonds that held communities and even families together" (Schama, *Embarrassment of Riches*, 92).

FIGURE 3. Franz Hals, *Portrait of a Dutch Family*, 1648.
Museo Thyssen-Bornemisza, Madrid.

to the natural disposition of man.[15] Involved through his patron,
Lord Cavendish, with the affairs of the Virginia Company that gov-
erned a colony in America, Hobbes accepted slavery as "an inevitable
part of the logic of power."[16] Even the inhabitants of "civil and flour-
ishing nations" could revert again to this state.[17] Hobbes was honest
and unconflicted about slavery—John Locke less so. The opening
sentence of book I, chapter I, of his *Two Treatises of Government* (1690)

15. Hobbes considered the "elemental struggle between two enemies" to be "the
natural condition which made slavery necessary as a social institution" (Davis, *Problem
of Slavery in Western Culture*, 120). Here Hobbes followed the earlier theorists, Samuel
Pufendorf and Hugo Grotius; the latter's book *War and Peace* (1853) included proslavery
views and the argument that slavery was legally acceptable.

16. Davis, *Problem of Slavery in the Age of Revolution*, 263.

17. Hulme, "The Spontaneous Hand of Nature," 24. Hulme is mainly concerned
with Hobbes's depiction of "savages" indigenous to the colonies.

states unequivocally:"Slavery is so vile and miserable an Estate of Man, and so directly opposite to the generous Temper and Courage of our Nation; that 'tis hardly to be conceived that an *Englishman,* much less a *Gentleman,* should plead for't."

But Locke's outrage against the "Chains for all Mankind" was not a protest against the enslavement of black Africans on New World plantations, least of all in colonies that were British.[18] Rather, slavery was a metaphor for legal tyranny, as it was used generally in British parliamentary debates on constitutional theory. A shareholder in the Royal African Company involved in American colonial policy in Carolina, Locke "clearly regarded Negro slavery a justifiable institution."[19] The isolation of the political discourse of social contract from the economy of household production (the *oikos*) made this double vision possible.[20] British liberty meant the protection of private property, and slaves were private property. So long as slaves fell under the jurisdiction of the household, their status was protected by law.[21]

18. Locke, *Two Treatises,* 141.

19. Davis, *Problem of Slavery in Western Culture,* 118. Locke was involved in the development of colonial policies through his patron, the Earl of Shaftesbury, and was a strong defender of the enterprise. He authored the Fundamental Constitutions of Carolina, sitting on its Council of Trade and Plantations as secretary from 1673 to 1675. The Carolina constitutions stated: "every freeman of Carolina, shall have absolute power and authority over his negro slaves" (Davis, *Problem of Slavery in Western Culture,* 118).

20. "In Locke's view, the origin of slavery, like the origin of liberty and property, was entirely outside the social contract" (Davis, *Problem of Slavery in Western Culture,* 119). Locke's philosophical argument tempered the universality of equality in the state of nature with the necessity of consent before a social contract could be undertaken, thereby excluding, explicitly, children and idiots from the contract, and by inference others who were uneducated or uneducable. See Mehta, "Liberal Strategies," 427–53.

21. Davis notes "the unfortunate fact that slaves were defined by law as property, and property was supposedly the foundation of liberty" (*Problem of Slavery in the Age of Revolution,* 267). It was only "after the Somerset decision of 1772" that "it was no longer possible to take for granted the universal legality of slave property" (*Problem of Slavery in the Age of Revolution,* 470), although William Davy, the lawyer in this case, argued for an earlier precedent: "In the eleventh year of Elizabeth's reign, Davy exclaimed, it had been resolved that '*England was too pure an Air for Slaves to breathe in.*'" Not so, writes Davis: "In point of fact, Negro slaves were bought and displayed in the courts of Elizabeth and her Stuart successors; they were publicly advertised for sale through most of the eighteenth century; and they were bequeathed in wills as late as the 1820s" (*Problem of Slavery in the*

4

A half-century later, the classical understanding of the economy—
and hence slave owning—as a private, household concern was bla-
tantly contradicted by new global realities. Sugar transformed the
West Indian colonial plantations. Both capital- and labor-intensive,
sugar production was protoindustrial, causing a precipitous rise in
the importation of African slaves and a brutal intensification of
their labor exploitation in order to meet a new and seemingly in-
satiable European demand for the addictive sweetness of sugar.[22]
Leading the Caribbean-wide sugar boom was the French colony of
Saint-Domingue that in 1767 produced 63,000 tons of sugar.[23]
Sugar production led to a seemingly infinite demand for slaves as
well, whose number in Saint-Domingue increased tenfold over the
eighteenth century to over 500,000 human beings. Within France,
more than 20 percent of the bourgeoisie was dependent upon
slave-connected commercial activity.[24] The French Enlightenment
thinkers wrote in the midst of this transformation. While they ide-
alized indigenous colonial populations with myths of the noble sav-
age (the "Indians" of the "New World"), the economic lifeblood of
slave labor was not their concern.[25] Although abolitionist movements

Age of Revolution, 472). When, in 1765, William Blackstone made the claim that "a slave
or negro, the moment he lands in England, falls under the protection of the laws, and
with regard to all natural rights becomes *eo instanti* a freeman," this did not apply to
slaves in the colonies. "Even Somerset's counsel conceded that English courts would
have to give effect to a contract for the purchase of slaves abroad" (*Problem of Slavery in the
Age of Revolution*, 473, 474).

22. See Mintz, *Sweetness and Power*.

23. See Davis, *Rise of the Atlantic Economies*, 257.

24. Louis Sala-Molins says one-third of the commercial activity in France de-
pended on the institution of slavery; see Sala-Molins, *Le Code Noir*, 244. More conser-
vative estimates put the figure at 20 percent.

25. It was Montesquieu who brought slavery into the Enlightenment discussion
and set the tone. While condemning the institution philosophically, he justified
"Negro" slavery on pragmatic, climatic, and blatantly racist grounds ("flat noses,"
"black from head to foot," and lacking in "common sense"). He concluded: "Weak
minds exaggerate too much the injustice done to Africans" by colonial slavery (Mon-
tesquieu, "Spirit of the Laws," 204).

FIGURE 4. Sir Peter Lely, *Elizabeth Countess of Dysart,* c. 1650. Ham House, Surrey. Slaves were fashionable in late seventeenth-century England, accompanying aristocratic ladies like household pets. The *London Advertiser* of 1756 "carried a notice by Matthew Dyer informing the public that he made 'silver padlocks for Blacks or Dogs; collars, etc.' . . . English ladies posed for their portraits either with their pet lamb, their pet lapdog or their pet black" (Dabydeen, *Hogarth's Blacks,* 21–23). Portraits by the Dutch-born Anthony van Dyck and Peter Lely were prototypes of a new genre of paintings, depicting black youths offering fruit and other symbols of wealth from the colonies to their owners. For the presence in Britain of slaves in the eighteenth century, see also Shyllon, *Black Slaves,* and Linebaugh, *London Hanged.*

FIGURE 5. Anthony van Dyck, *Henrietta of Lorraine*, 1634.
Kenwood House.

did exist at this time, and in France the Amis des Noirs (Friends of the Blacks) decried the excesses of slavery, a defense of liberty on the grounds of racial equality was rare indeed.[26]

"Man is born free, and everywhere he is in chains." So writes Jean-Jacques Rousseau in the opening lines of *On the Social Contract*, first published in 1762.[27] No human condition appears more offensive to his heart or to his reason than slavery. And yet even Rousseau, patron saint of the French Revolution, represses from consciousness the millions of really existing, European-owned slaves, as he relentlessly condemns the institution. Rousseau's egregious omission has been scrupulously exposed by scholarship, but only recently. The Catalonian-born philosopher Louis Sala-Molins has written a history (1987) of Enlightenment thought through the lens of *Le Code Noir*, the French legal code that applied to black slaves in the colonies, drawn up in 1685 and signed by Louis XIV and not definitively eradicated until 1848. Sala-Molins proceeds point by point through the code, which legalized not only slavery, the treatment of human beings as moveable property, but the branding, torture, physical mutilation, and killing of slaves for attempting to defy their inhuman status. He juxtaposes this code, which applied to all slaves under French jurisdiction, to the Enlightenment philosophers' texts, documenting their indignation regarding slavery in theory while "superbly" ignoring slavery in practice. Sala-Molins is outraged and rightly so. In the *Social Contract*, Rousseau argues:

26. Most frequently cited as an exception was the work of a priest, the Abbé Raynal, whose book (written with the collaboration of Diderot) *Histoire philosophique et politique des établissements et du commerce des Européens dans les deux Indes* (1770) predicted a black Spartacus who would arise in the New World to avenge the rights of nature. The book was widely read, and not only in Europe; Toussaint-Louverture himself was inspired by it. See James, *Black Jacobins*, 24–25. Michel-Rolph Trouillot has cautioned against too sanguine a reading of this passage, however, which was contextualized as a warning to Europeans, rather than an appeal to the slaves themselves: "It was not a clear prediction of a Louverture-type character, as some would want with hindsight. . . . The most radical stance is in the unmistakable reference to a single human species" (Trouillot, *Silencing the Past*, 85).

27. Rousseau, *Basic Political Writings*, 141.

"The right of slavery is null, not simply because it is illegitimate, but because it is absurd and meaningless. These words, *slavery* and *right* [*droit,* that is, law], are contradictory. They are mutually exclusive."[28] Sala-Molins makes us see the consequences of this statement: "The *Code Noir,* the most perfect example of this kind of convention in the time of Rousseau, is not a legal code. The right of which it speaks is not a right, as it claims to make legal that which cannot be legalized, slavery."[29] He thus finds it preposterous that Rousseau never in his writings mentions the *Code Noir.* "The one existing, flagrant case of what he is declaring categorically untenable gets none of his attention."[30] Sala-Molins scrutinizes the texts for any evidence that might excuse this silence and finds, unequivocally, that Rousseau knew the facts. The Enlightenment philosopher cited travel literature of the time—Kolben on the Hottentots, du Tertre on Indians in the Antilles—but avoided those pages of these same accounts that describe the horrors of European slavery explicitly. Rousseau referred to human beings everywhere—but omitted Africans; spoke of Greenland's people transported to Denmark who die of sadness—but not of the sadness of Africans transported to the Indies that resulted in suicides, mutinies, and maroonings. He declared all men equal and saw private property as the source of inequality, but he never put two and two together to discuss French slavery for economic profit as central to arguments of both equality and property.[31] As in the Dutch Republic and Britain, African slaves were present, used and abused domestically within France.[32] Indeed, Rousseau could not *not* have known "that there are boudoirs in Paris where one

28. Rousseau, *Basic Political Writings,* 146.

29. Sala-Molins, *Le Code Noir,* 238.

30. Sala-Molins, *Le Code Noir,* 241. Rather, Rousseau's examples are from ancient times, for example, Braidas of Sparta against the satrap of Persepolis! See Rousseau, *Basic Political Writings,* 72.

31. See Sala-Molins, *Le Code Noir,* 243–46

32. See Cohen, *French Encounter with Africans.* In 1764, the French government prohibited entry of blacks into the metropolis. In 1777, the law was modified to lift some of the restrictions, allowing colonial slaves to accompany their masters.

amuses oneself indiscriminately with a monkey and a young black boy (*négrillon*)."[33]

Sala-Molins pronounces Rousseau's silence in the face of this evidence "racist" and "revolting."[34] Such outrage is unusual among scholars who, as professionals, are trained to avoid passionate judgments in their writing. This moral neutrality is built into the disciplinary methods that, while based on a variety of philosophical premises, result in the same exclusions. Today's intellectual historian who treats Rousseau in context will follow good professional form by relativizing the situation, judging (and excusing) Rousseau's racism by the mores of his time, in order to avoid thereby the fallacy of anachronism. Or, today's philosopher, who is trained to analyze theory totally abstracted from historical context, will attribute a universality to Rousseau's writings that transcends the author's own intent or personal limitations in order to avoid thereby the fallacy of reduction ad hominem. In both cases, the embarrassing facts are quietly allowed to disappear. They are visible, however, in general histories of the era, where they cannot help but be mentioned because when Enlightenment theory was put into practice, the perpetrators of political revolutions stumbled over the economic fact of slavery in ways that made their own acknowledgment of the contradiction impossible to avoid.

5

The colonial revolutionaries of America fighting for their independence against Britain mobilized Locke's political discourse to their ends. The metaphor of slavery was central to that struggle but

---

33. Sala-Molins, *Le Code Noir*, 248.

34. Sala-Molins, *Le Code Noir*, 253. The author as well of *L'Afrique aux Amériques*, Sala-Molins points out that the Spanish priest Bartoleme de Las Casas, who protested against slavery of indigenous American Indians (if not Africans) in the sixteenth century, was in significant ways more progressive than the secular *philosophes* two centuries later.

in a new sense: "Americans genuinely believed that men who were taxed without their consent were literally slaves, since they had lost the power to resist oppression, and since defenselessness inevitably led to tyranny."[35] In evoking the liberties of natural rights theory, the American colonists as slave owners were led to "a monstrous inconsistency."[36] And, yet, although some, like Benjamin Rush, acknowledged their bad faith,[37] and some, like Thomas Jefferson, blamed black slavery on the British;[38] although the slaves themselves petitioned for their liberty,[39] and a few individual states passed antislavery legislation,[40] the new nation, conceived in liberty, tolerated the "monstrous inconsistency," writing slavery into the United States Constitution.

35. Davis, *Problem of Slavery in the Age of Revolution*, 273. Davis is citing Bernard Bailyn in this case. I am following Davis's presentation closely here.

36. Jordan, *White over Black,* 289. Their enemies, the British Tories, seized upon this: "'How is it,' asked Samuel Johnson, 'that we hear the loudest *yelps* for liberty among the drivers of negroes?'" (Davis, *Problem of Slavery in Western Culture*, 3).

37. "The plant of liberty is of so tender a Nature, that it cannot thrive long in the neighborhood of slavery" (Benjamin Rush [1773], quoted in Davis, *Problem of Slavery in the Age of Revolution*, 283).

38. In a suppressed clause of the Declaration of Independence, Thomas Jefferson charged that the British King George III

"has waged cruel war against human nature itself, violating the most sacred rights of life and liberty in the persons of a distant people who never offended him, captivating and carrying them into slavery in another hemisphere . . . determined to keep open a market where MEN should be bought and sold. . . . He is now exciting these very people to rise in arms among us, and to purchase that liberty of which *he* deprived them, by murdering the people upon whom *he* also intruded them, thus paying off former crimes committed against the *liberties* of one people, with crimes that he urges them to commit against the *lives* of another." (Davis, *Problem of Slavery in the Age of Revolution*, 273)

39. "We have in common with all other men . . . a naturel right to our freedoms without Being depriv'd of them by our fellow men as we are a freeborn Pepel and have never forfeited this Blessing by aney compact or agreement whatever" (quoted in Davis, *Problem of Slavery in the Age of Revolution*, 276).

40. If the American Revolution could not solve the problem of slavery, it at least led to a *perception* of the problem. Nor was the desire for consistency a matter of empty rhetoric. It appeared in the antislavery resolutions of New England town meetings, in the Vermont constitution of 1777, in individual wills that manumitted slaves, in Rhode Island's law of 1774 that prohibited future importation of slaves, and in Pennsylvania's gradual emancipation act of 1780, adopted, according to a preamble written by Thomas Paine, "in grateful commemoration of our own happy deliverance" from British occupation (Davis, *Problem of Slavery in the Age of Revolution*, 285–86).

The French encyclopedist, Denis Diderot, spoke admiringly of the U.S. revolutionaries as having "burned their chains" and "refused slavery."[41] But if the colonial nature of the United States' struggle for freedom made it somehow possible to sustain the distinction between the political discourse and social institutions, in the case of the French Revolution a decade later the various meanings of slavery became hopelessly entangled when they came up against fundamental contradictions between revolutionary developments within France and developments in the French colonies without. It took years of bloodshed before slavery—really-existing slavery, not merely its metaphorical analogy—was abolished in the French colonies, and even then the gains were only temporary. Although abolition of slavery was the only possible logical outcome of the ideal of universal freedom, it did not come about through the revolutionary ideas or even the revolutionary actions of the French; it came about through the actions of the slaves themselves. The epicenter of this struggle was the colony of Saint-Domingue. In 1791, while even the most ardent opponents of slavery within France dragged their feet, the half-million slaves in Saint-Domingue, the richest colony not only of France but of the entire colonial world, took the struggle for liberty into their own hands, not through petitions, but through violent, organized revolt.[42] In 1794, the armed

41. Trouillot, *Silencing the Past*, 85. The *Encyclopédie* edited by Diderot and D'Alembert, included entries concerning really existing slavery. Although the article entitled "Nègres" observed simply that their labor "is indispensable for the cultivation of sugar, tobacco, indigo, etc.," a series of entries by Jaucourt was forceful: "Esclavage" declared slavery contrary to nature; "Liberté naturelle" accused religion of using its pretext against natural right because slaves were needed for the colonies, plantations, and mines; "Traité des Nègres" declared slaves traded to be "illicit merchandise—prohibited by all the laws of humanity and equality," so that abolition was necessary even if it ruined the colonies: "Let the colonies be destroyed rather than be the cause of so much evil." But racism was still present in these texts (Sala-Molins, *Le Code Noir*, 254–61), and abolition was advised as a gradual process in order to prepare the slaves for freedom.

42. This slave conspiracy was led by Boukman, a priest of Vodou, a new syncretic cult that not only brought together slaves from diverse cultures of Africa, but included Western cultural symbols as well (see below, note 129). Boukman addressed the slaves:

blacks of Saint-Domingue forced the French Republic to acknowl-
edge the fait accompli of the abolition of slavery on that island
(declared by the French colonial commissioners, Sonthonax and
Polverel, acting on their own) and to universalize abolition through-
out the French colonies.[43] From 1794 to 1800, as freemen, these
former slaves engaged in a struggle against invading British forces,
who many of the white and mulatto land-owning colonists of Saint-
Domingue hoped would reestablish slavery.[44] The black army under
the leadership of Toussaint Louverture defeated the British militar-
ily in a struggle that strengthened the Abolitionist movement within
Britain, setting the stage for the British suspension of the slave trade
in 1807.[45] In 1801, Toussaint Louverture, the former slave and now
governor of Saint-Domingue, suspected that the French Directory

---

"Throw away the symbol of the god of the whites who has so often caused us to weep, and
listen to the voice of liberty, which speaks in the hearts of us all" (James, *Black Jacobins*,
87). Although slave rebellions had occurred in Saint-Domingue with great regularity
(1679, 1713, 1720, 1730, 1758, 1777, 1782, and 1787, before the massive revolt in 1791;
see Dupuy, *Haiti*, 34), within the context of the radicalization of the French Revolution,
Boukman's uprising changed Europeans' perception of slave revolts—no longer one of
a long series of slave rebellions, but an extension of the European Revolution: "News
of the summer of 1791 had focused on the flight to Varennes and capture of the French
royal family *and* on the revolt of the slaves in Santo Domingo" (Paulson, *Representations
of Revolution*, 93).

43. Slavery was abolished by Polverel and Sonthonax in August 1793, acting in-
dependently of orders from Paris. The role of both men has been neglected by scholars,
another case of scholarly blindness that, to use Trouillot's felicitous term, "silences
the past"(see Trouillot, *Silencing the Past*). See the recent symposium edited by Marcel
Dorigny, *Léger-Félicité Sonthonax*, which begins to redress this situation; in particular, see
Desné, "Sonthonax vu par les dictionnaires," 113–20, which traces the almost total
disappearance of Sonthonax's name from the bibliographical encyclopedias of France
in the course of the twentieth century.

44. The British were compelled pragmatically to grant freedom to those slaves of
Saint-Domingue who agreed to fight on their side—as did Sonthonax and Polverel in
the case of those fighting for the French Republic. The effect of these policies was to
undermine slavery by contradicting any ontological argument that the slaves were in-
capable of freedom; see Geggus, "British Occupation of Saint Domingue," 363.

45. Geggus notes: "The part played by Haiti in the anti-slavery movement's sud-
den resurgence in 1804 seems to have been entirely ignored in the scholarly literature.
Yet its importance was apparently considerable" (Geggus, "Haiti and the Abolitionists,"
116). Again, here is a case of scholarly blindness that silences the past.

might attempt to rescind abolition.[46] And yet, still loyal to the republic,[47] he wrote a constitution for the colony that was in advance of any such document in the world—if not in its premises of democracy, then surely in regard to the racial inclusiveness of its definition of the citizenry.[48] In 1802, Napoleon did move to reestablish slavery and the *Code Noir* and had Toussaint arrested and deported to France, where he died in prison in 1803. When Napoleon sent French troops under Leclerc to subdue the colony, waging a brutal struggle against the black population "that amounted to a war of genocide,"[49] the black citizens of Saint-Domingue once again took up arms, demonstrating, in Leclerc's own words: "It is not enough to have taken away Toussaint, there are 2,000 leaders to be taken away."[50] On 1 January 1804, the new military leader, slave-born Jean-Jacques Dessalines, took the final step of declaring independ-

46. In 1796, General Laveaux appointed Toussaint governor, and hailed him as savior of the republic and redeemer of the slaves predicted by Raynal; see Blackburn, *Overthrow of Colonial Slavery*, 233. In 1802, the *Code Noir* was reestablished in Martinique and Guadeloupe (although nothing was said about Saint-Domingue).

47. Louverture had allied himself earlier with the King of Spain, setting up military operations and working in the eastern half of the island, which was a Spanish colony; but once he learned that the French Assembly had abolished slavery, he joined with Sonthonax against the British and was loyal to the French Republic until his arrest. (This change of alliances, which has been a point of controversy, is analyzed by Geggus, "'From His Most Catholic Majesty,'" 488–89.)

48. To aid him in drawing up a constitution, Toussaint summoned an assembly of six men (including the Bordeaux-raised, mulatto lawyer Julien Raimond; more on him below):

> The Constitution is Toussaint L'Ouverture from the first line to the last, and in it he enshrined his principles of government. Slavery was forever abolished. Every man, whatever his colour, was admissible to all employments, and there was to exist no other distinction than that of virtues and talents, and no other superiority than that which the law gives in the exercise of a public function. He incorporated in the Constitution an article which preserved their rights to all proprietors absent from the colony "for whatever reason" except if they were on the list of émigrés proscribed in France. For the rest, Toussaint concentrated all power in his own hands. (James, *Black Jacobins*, 263)

Toussaint's regime anticipated dominion status. France missed this chance to establish a policy of enlightened imperialism.

49. Geggus, "Slavery, War, and Revolution," 22.

50. James, *Black Jacobins*, 346.

ence from France, thus combining the end of slavery with the end of colonial status. Under the banner of Liberty or Death (these words were inscribed on the red and blue flag, from which the white band of the French had been removed),[51] he defeated the French troops and destroyed the white population, establishing in 1805 an independent, constitutional nation of "black" citizens, an "empire," mirroring Napoleon's own, which he called by the Arawak name, Haiti.[52] These events, leading to the complete freedom of the slaves and the colony, were unprecedented. "Never before had a slave society successfully overthrown its ruling class."[53]

The self-liberation of the African slaves of Saint-Domingue gained for them, by force, the recognition of European and American whites—if only in the form of fear. Among those with egalitarian sympathies, it gained them respect as well. For almost a decade, before the violent elimination of whites signalled their deliberate retreat from universalist principles, the black Jacobins of Saint-Domingue surpassed the metropole in actively realizing the Enlightenment goal of human liberty, seeming to give proof that the French Revolution was not simply a European phenomenon but world-historical in its implications.[54] If we have become accustomed to different narratives, ones that place colonial events on the margins of European history, we have been seriously misled.

51. See James, *Black Jacobins*, 365. Writing under a pseudonym in a Boston newspaper in support of the Saint-Domingue revolution, Abraham Bishop "remarked that the American revolutionaries who had taught the world to echo the cry 'Liberty or Death!' did not say 'all *white* men *are free,* but *all men* are free'" (Davis, *Revolutions,* 50).

52. Dessalines's constitution declared *all* Haitians black, attempting to legislate away the categories of mulatto and various gradients of interraciality. Dessalines was assassinated in 1806; Haiti was then divided into two parts, a north "kingdom," headed by Henri Christophe, and a south "republic," the president of which was Alexandre Pétion.

53. Geggus, "Haiti and the Abolitionists," 114

54. Trouillot calls the Haitian Revolution "the most radical political revolution of that age" (*Silencing the Past,* 98). Blackburn writes: "Haiti was not the first independent American state but it was the first to guarantee civic liberty to all its inhabitants" (*Overthrow of Colonial Slavery,* 260).

Events in Saint-Domingue were central to contemporary attempts to make sense out of the reality of the French Revolution and its aftermath.[55] We need to be aware of the facts from this perspective.

6

Let us consider the logical unfolding of the overthrow of slavery in terms of the evolution in consciousness of Europeans living through it. The French revolutionaries understood themselves from the start as a liberation movement that would free people from the "slavery" of feudal inequities. In 1789, the slogans Live Freely or Die and Rather Death Than Slavery were common, and the "Marseillaise" denounced "l'esclavage antique" in this context.[56] This was a revolution against, not merely the tyranny of a particular ruler, but of all past traditions that violated the general principles of human liberty. Reporting on the events in Paris in summer 1789, the German publicist Johann Wilhelm von Archenholz (from whom we will hear again) lost his customary journalistic neutrality and exclaimed that the French "people" (*Volk*), who "were accustomed to kissing their chains . . . had, in a matter of hours, broken these gigantic chains with one all-conquering stroke of courage, becoming freer than the Romans and Greeks were, and the Americans and British are today."[57]

55. Was the French Revolution a "mere reform of abuses," as Napoleon claimed the English considered it, or did it constitute "a complete social rebirth," as he was to say on his deathbed (Paulson, *Representations of Revolution*, 51)? At the end of his life, Napoleon regretted his treatment of Toussaint Louverture.

56. Blackburn, *Overthrow of Colonial Slavery*, 230.

57. Cited in Ruof, *Johann Wilhelm von Archenholtz*, 29. (Ruof's spelling of the name as "Archenholtz" is unusual.) Archenholz continued: "They should be honored by the German people, who thereby honor themselves" (*Johann Wilhelm von Archenholtz*, 30). In 1792 he again used the metaphor of slavery in describing the French revolutionary situation, asking whether the people of "one of the most populous nations on earth, that in the past few years had climbed out of the deepest slime of slavery, and . . . tasted the sweet fruits of freedom to the point of overfullness . . . so soon again would quietly bow their necks under the yoke, regarding their broken chains as playthings. . . . Even the combined might of Europe would be wrecked against this rock" (*Johann Wilhelm von Archenholtz*, 49).

But what of the colonies, the source of wealth of such a large part of the French population? The meaning of freedom was at stake in their reaction to the events of 1789 and nowhere more so than in the crown jewel, Saint-Domingue. Would the colonists take after the Americans and revolt, as some of the Creole planters of Saint-Domingue were urging? Or would they join fraternally to proclaim their "liberty" as French citizens? And if the latter, then who were to be included as citizens? Property owners, to be sure.[58] But only whites? Mulattoes owned an estimated one-third of the cultivated land in Saint-Domingue.[59] Ought not they to be included, and not only they, but the free blacks as well? Was property or was race the litmus test for being a citizen of France? Most pertinent, if Africans could in principle be included as citizens—if, that is, the implicitly racist assumptions that underlay the *Code Noir* were not valid—then how could the continued legal enslavement of blacks be justified?[60] And if it could not, how could the colonial system be maintained? The unfolding of the logic of freedom in the colonies threatened to unravel the total institutional framework of the slave economy that supported such a substantial part of the French bourgeoisie, whose political revolution, of course, this was.[61]

58. In 1790, a colonial assembly in Saint-Domingue extended the vote to non-propertied whites (widening the franchise further than in the metropole), hence reinforcing the racial nature of political exclusion; see Blackburn, *Overthrow of Colonial Slavery*, 183.

59. Blackburn writes that they owned 2,000 coffee estates in the west and south, compared with 780 sugar estates, the great majority of which were owned by whites: "In St. Domingue free people of colour were almost as numerous as white colonists, indeed possibly more numerous." The proprietors of color owned about 100,000 slaves: "nowhere else in the Americas did those of partly African descent figure so importantly in the ranks of the propertied class"; they often "bore the distinguished name of a French father" (*Overthrow of Colonial Slavery*, 168, 169).

60. The Baron de Wimpffen asked if colonists were not afraid to say *liberty* or *equality* in front of their slaves; see James, *Black Jacobins*, 82. But it was still rare in 1792 for republicans to declare forcefully, as did Sonthonax, "'One cannot maintain the Blacks in slavery if free men who are equal to the Whites are also black like the slaves'" (Thibau, "Saint-Domingue à l'arrivée de Sonthonax," 44).

61. In the Constituent Assembly (1789–91), consisting of approximately 1,100 deputies, one in ten had interests in Saint-Domingue; see Thibau, "Saint-Domingue à l'arrivée de Sonthonax," 41.

And yet only the logic of freedom gave legitimacy to their revolution in the universal terms in which the French saw themselves.

The Haitian Revolution was the crucible, the trial by fire for the ideals of the French Enlightenment. And every European who was part of the bourgeois reading public knew it.[62] "The eyes of the world are now on St. Domingo."[63] So begins an article published in 1804 in *Minerva,* the journal founded by Archenholz, who had been covering the French Revolution since its beginnings and reporting on the revolution in Saint-Domingue since 1792.[64] For a full year, from fall 1804 to the end of 1805, *Minerva* published a continuing series, totalling more than a hundred pages, including source documents, news summaries, and eyewitness accounts, that informed its readers not only of the final struggle for independence of this French colony—under the banner Liberty or Death![65]—but of events

62. The Amis des Noirs (founded in 1788) were important in setting the stage for this discussion. Although not great in numbers, they were influential as writers and pamphleteers (Condorcet, Brissot, Mirabeau, the Abbé Grégoire), whose work deplored the conditions of the colonial slaves. Marcus Rainsford wrote in 1805 that as a result of their circulated writings, negro slaves "were the prominent subjects of conversation and regret in half the towns of Europe"; as they, with "unhappy eloquence" depicted "the miseries of slavery," and "were certainly the cause of bringing into action, on a broad basis, that spirit of revolt which only sleeps in the enslaved African, or his descendent" (Rainsford, *Historical Account,* 107). The position of the Amis des Noirs was to endorse only gradual emancipation, until 1791, when they endorsed rights for free blacks and mulattoes; by the time of the actual abolition of slavery (1794) they had ceased to exist, victims of Robespierre's purges. Abolition had come to be identified with Robespierre's enemies the Girondins: "The Girondins were accused of having secretly fomented the colonial upheavals to the advantage of England and of supporting abolition in order to ruin France's empire. . . . Robespierre himself was conspicuously absent during the February 4 session [of the Convention, which voted unanimously to abolish slavery] and did not sign the decree" (Fick, "French Revolution in Saint Domingue," 68; compare with Bénot, "Comment la Convention a-t-elle voté l'abolition," 13–25).

63. Archenholz, "Zur neuesten Geschichte von St. Domingo," 340. This was Archenholz's editorial introduction to the 1804 article in *Minerva* (341–45), which was critical of the revolution's violence and skeptical of the viability of the "negro-state."

64. See "Historische Nachrichten von den letzten Unruhen in Saint Domingo: Aus verschiedenen Quellen gezogen," *Minerva* 1 (Feb. 1792): 296–319. The article favored mulatto rights, the position of Brissot, and the Amis des Noirs.

65. This slogan, proclaimed by Dessalines in May 1803, was reported in Archenholz, "Zur neuesten Geschichte von St. Domingo," 506.

over the previous ten years as well. Archenholz was critical of the violence of this revolution (as he was of the Jacobin Terror in the metropole), but he came to appreciate Toussaint Louverture, publishing as part of his series, in German translation, a chapter from the new manuscript by a British captain, Marcus Rainsford, who praised Toussaint's character, leadership, and humanity in superlatives.[66]

Archenholz's journal borrowed freely from English and French sources so that his account reflected news widely reported to the European reading public, and the articles in *Minerva* were picked up in turn by "countless newspapers" (a situation of cosmopolitan and open communication, despite intellectual property restrictions, that has perhaps not been matched until the early Internet).[67] Although there was censorship in the French press after 1803,[68]

---

66. Rainsford's book, published in England in 1805 (and in full German translation the following year) asserted:

> The rise of the Haytian Empire may powerfully affect the condition of the human race. . . . It will scarcely be credited in another age, that philosophers heard unmoved, of the ascertainment of a brilliant fact, hitherto unknown, or confined to the vague knowledge of those whose experience is not admitted within the pale of historical truth. . . . It is on ancient record, that negroes were capable of repelling their enemies, with vigour, in their own country; and a writer of modern date [Adanson, *Voyage á L'Afrique,* 1749–53] has assured us of the talents and virtues of these people; but it remained for the close of the eighteenth century to realize the scene, from a state of abject degeneracy:— to exhibit, a horde of negroes emancipating themselves from the vilest slavery, and at once filling the relations of society, enacting laws, and commanding armies, in the colonies of Europe. The same period has witnessed a great and polished nation [France] . . . returning to the barbarism of the earliest periods. (*Historical Account,* x–xi)

Rainsford ranked the Haitian Revolution "among the most remarkable and important transactions of the day" (*Historical Account,* 364).

67. Ruof, *Johann Wilhelm von Archenholtz,* 62.

68. "Abolitionism, always an affair of small cliques in France, now effectively ceased to exist. The attempt to reconquer Saint Domingue had been accompanied by a flood of literature concerning the colony, but it was largely the work of colonists who, with varying degrees of vituperation, blamed the black revolution on abolitionist influence. Then, as the Saint Domingue expedition came entirely to grief, a total ban was imposed on all works concerning the colonies" (Geggus, "Haiti and the Abolitionists," 117).

newspapers and journals in Britain (also the United States and Poland)[69] highlighted the events of the final revolutionary struggle in Saint-Domingue—the *Edinburgh Review,* among others.[70] William Wordsworth wrote a sonnet entitled "To Toussaint Louverture," published in the *Morning Post* in February 1803, in which he deplored the reestablishment of the *Code Noir* in the French colonies.[71]

In the German-language press, *Minerva's* coverage was special. Already in 1794, two years after its founding, it had established its reputation as the best of its genre of political journals. It strove to be nonpartisan, objective, and factual, aiming at "historical truth" that would be "instructive . . . [for] our grandchildren."[72] Its goal, according to the journal's (English!) motto, was "to shew the very age and body of the time its form and pressure."[73] By 1798, its circulation was three thousand copies (respectable in *our* day for an intellectually serious journal), and that number is estimated to have doubled by 1809. In the words of Archenholz's biographer, *Minerva*

69. The U.S. press was full of the story of Saint-Domingue. John Adams, while lamenting the events, believed that they were the logical outcome of what the U.S. rebellion itself had caused. Others saw the slave revolution as proof that slavery needed to be abolished in the United States—in other words, both sides read it as significant for *world* history; see Davis, *Revolutions,* 49–54. War correspondents also sent reports back regularly to Polish newspapers, as a Polish regiment was part of the military force under General Leclerc sent by Napoleon to reestablish slavery in Saint-Domingue. See Pachonski and Wilson, *Poland's Caribbean Tragedy.*

70. See Geggus, "Haiti and the Abolitionists," 113–15. In fact most of the reporting was not very favorable, with the exception of heroization of Toussaint Louverture.

71. The sonnet was "probably written in France in August 1802" (Geggus, "British Opinion," 140). Wordsworth was born the same year as Hegel (1770); both were in their early thirties at this time. William Blake also incorporated the Haitian revolution into his poetry.

72. Ruof, *Johann Wilhelm von Archenholtz,* 69–70. Archenholz declared the "strictest neutrality" (*strengste Unparteilichkeit*) to be his "first duty" (*Johann Wilhelm von Archenholtz,* 40).

73. This appeared on the title page. Note that scholars of *Minerva* need to go back to the original journal to discover the intense interest of Archenholz in Saint-Domingue and the Haitian Revolution. The two monographs that have been written on him do not mention these articles; see Ruof, *Johann Wilhelm von Archenholtz,* and Rieger, *Johann Wilhelm von Archenholz als "Zeitbürger."* But see Schüller, *Die Deutsche Rezeption haitianischer*

was "the most important political journal of the turn of the century" both in terms of quality of content, written by regular correspondents (who were important public figures in their own right), and the quality of readers, among whom were some of the most influential people in Germany.[74] King Friedrich Wilhelm III of Prussia "read *Minerva* constantly."[75] Both Goethe and Schiller read *Minerva* (the latter corresponded with Archenholz),[76] as well as Klopstock (who contributed to the journal), Schelling, and Lafayette. And—need I keep it from you any longer?—another regular reader of *Minerva,* as we know from his published letters, was the philosopher Georg Wilhelm Friedrich Hegel.[77]

Geschichte, which includes a summary of the *Minerva* articles on Saint-Domingue as well as a discussion of the accounts of the Haitian Revolution in other German journals and books, including the very influential German translation of Rainsford (103–8). Schüller's book was brought to my attention by Geggus after the writing of this paper, and I have added references to it in the notes when appropriate.

74. Ruof, *Johann Wilhelm von Archenholtz,* 131. Two particularly well-known correspondents were Konrad Engelbert Olsner and Georg Forster; more on them below. For circulation figures, see Ruof, *Johann Wilhelm von Archenholtz,* 129–30.

75. Ruof, *Johann Wilhelm von Archenholtz,* 130.

76. Schiller wrote to Archenholz in 1794, suggesting that he do a retrospective on the American Revolution in the journal: "Ist es Ihnen noch nicht die Idee gekommen, ein kurzes, gedrängtes tableau von den amerikanischen Freiheitskriege aufzustellen?" (Ruof, *Johann Wilhelm von Archenholtz,* 45). Although no such article appeared in *Minerva,* the series on the Saint-Domingue events, 1791–1805, was analogous in its conception.

77. Hegel wrote to Schelling from Bern, Christmas Eve, 1794: "Quite by accident I spoke a few days ago with the author of the letters signed 'O.' in Archenholz's *Minerva.* You are no doubt acquainted with them. The author, purportedly an Englishman, is in fact a Silesian named Oeslner . . . still a young man, but one sees that he has toiled much" (Hegel, *Hegel: The Letters,.* 28). Ruof (writing in 1915) does not mention Hegel as a reader of *Minerva.* The German publication of Hegel's letters was not available to him; see Hegel, *Briefe von und an Hegel.* Jacques d'Hont, however, begins his book with a chapter on the influence of *Minerva* on Hegel (and Schelling), which he describes as "total" (*globale*) (*Hegel Secret,* 7–43). Note that d'Hont makes no mention of the articles on Saint-Domingue that appeared in *Minerva's* pages (his point is a different one; see below, note 121). Konrad Engelbert Oelsner, more radically republican than Archenholz, was an (anti-Robespierrean) Girondist; his hero was the Abbé Sieyès. See his history of the French Revolution (based on his eyewitness reports) *Luzifer.*

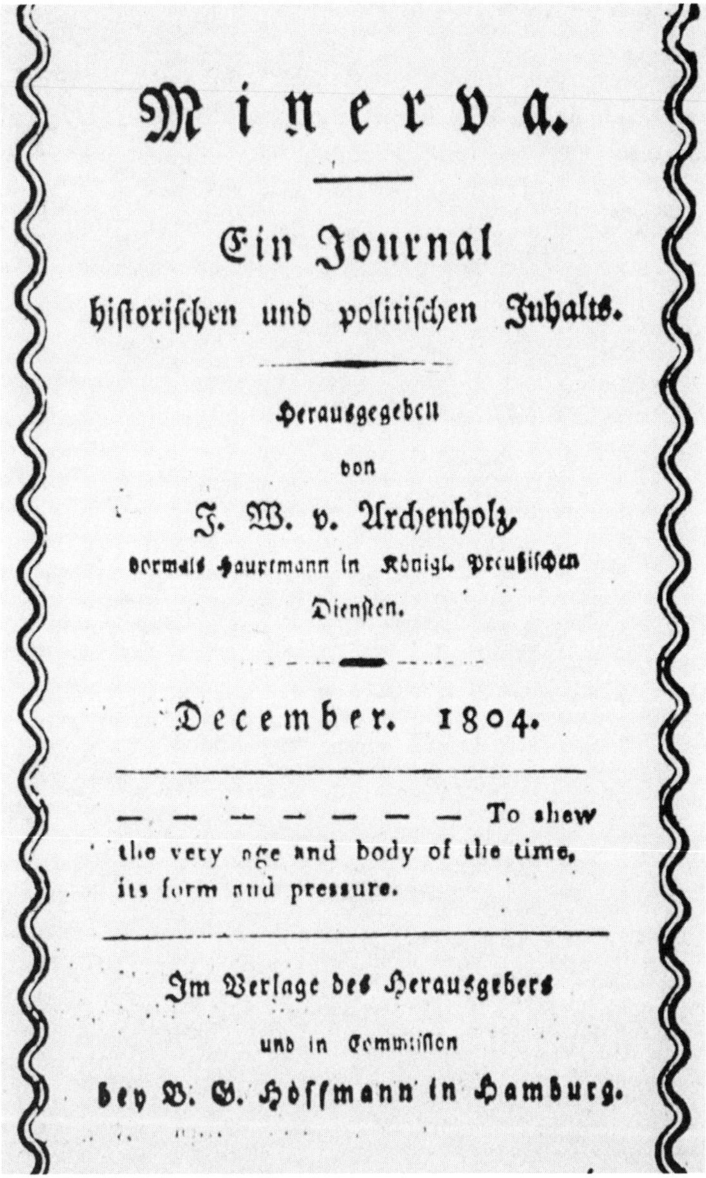

Minerva.

Ein Journal
historischen und politischen Inhalts.

Herausgegeben

von

J. W. v. Archenholz,
vormals Hauptmann in Königl. Preußischen
Diensten.

December. 1804.

— — — — — — — — To shew
the very age and body of the time,
its form and pressure.

Im Verlage des Herausgebers

und in Commission

bey B. G. Hoffmann in Hamburg.

FIGURE 6. Cover page of *Minerva*.

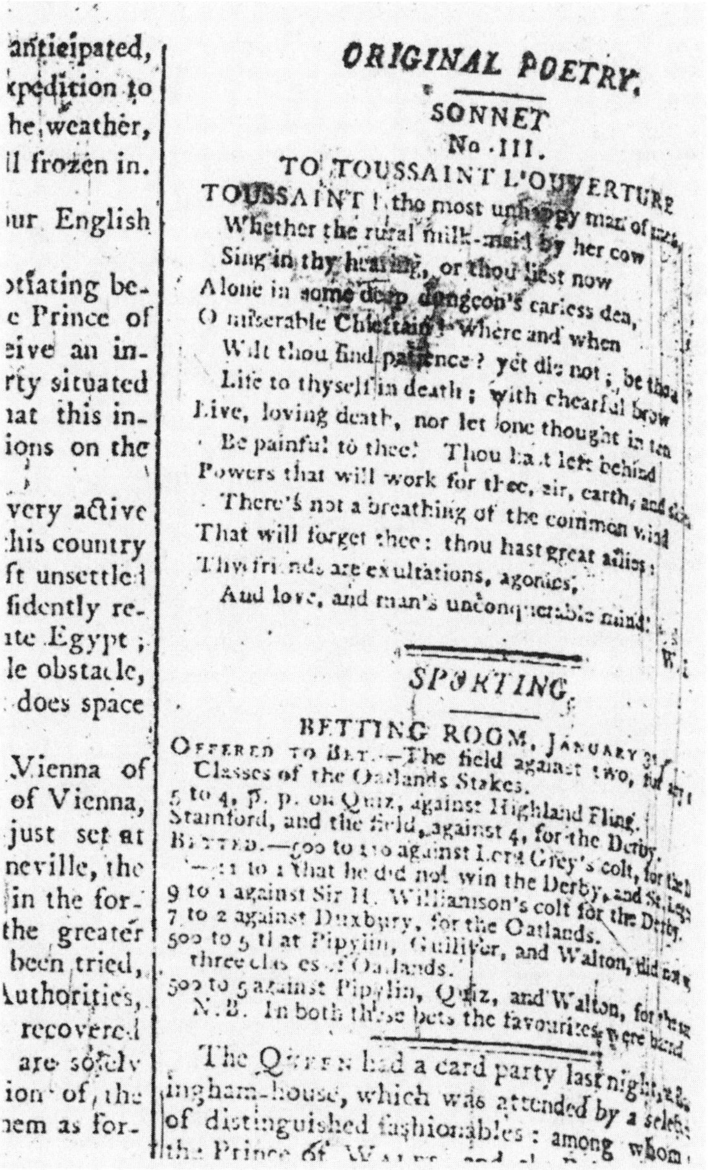

ORIGINAL POETRY.

SONNET
No. III.
TO TOUSSAINT L'OUVERTURE.

TOUSSAINT! tho most unhappy man of men!
Whether the rural milk-maid by her cow
Sing in thy hearing, or thou liest now
Alone in some deep dungeon's earless den,
O miserable Chieftain! where and when
Wilt thou find patience? yet die not; be thou
Life to thyself in death; with chearful brow
Live, loving death, nor let one thought in ten
Be painful to thee! Thou hast left behind
Powers that will work for thee, air, earth, and skies;
There's not a breathing of the common wind
That will forget thee: thou hast great allies;
Thy friends are exultations, agonies,
And love, and man's unconquerable mind.

W.

SPORTING

BETTING ROOM, January 31.

FIGURE 7. Wordsworth's sonnet *Morning Post*, 2 February 1803.

7

"Where did Hegel's idea of the relation between lordship and bondage originate?" ask the Hegel experts, repeatedly, referring to the famous metaphor of the "struggle to death" between the master and slave, which for Hegel provided the key to the unfolding of freedom in world history and which he first elaborated in *The Phenomenology of Mind,* written in Jena in 1805–6 (the first year of the Haitian nation's existence) and published in 1807 (the year of the British abolition of the slave trade). Where, indeed? The intellectual historians of German philosophy know only one place to look for the answer: the writings of other intellectuals. Perhaps it was Fichte, writes George Armstrong Kelly, although "the problem of lordship and bondage is essentially Platonic."[78] Judith Shklar takes the common route of connecting Hegel's discussion to Aristotle. Otto Pöggeler—and there is no finer name in German Hegel scholarship —says that the metaphor does not come from even the ancients, but is a totally "abstract" example.[79] Only one scholar, Pierre-Franklin Tavarès, has ever actually made the connection of Hegel and Haiti, basing his argument on evidence that Hegel read the French abolitionist, the Abbé Grégoire.[80] (His work, written in the early 1990s,

78. Kelly, "Hegel's 'Lordship and Bondage,'" 260. Kelly insists that Hegel's writings have to be considered within "Hegel's own time," but it is a time of thought ("Hegel's 'Lordship and Bondage,'" 272). He considers therefore the philosophical differences between Fichte, Schelling, and Hegel: Fichte's thematic was the more general one of mutual recognition (a theme Hegel had treated earlier), whereas in the master-slave dialectic "Hegel is defending a doctrine of original equality that is curiously and dangerously denied by Fichte" ("Hegel's 'Lordship and Bondage,'" 269). Many interpreters choose to discuss Hegel on this point in terms of Fichte, thereby reducing the importance of Hegel's specific example of recognition first introduced in 1803, the relationship of master and slave. See, for example, Williams (who in turn follows Ludwig Siep): "The story of recognition is a story about Fichte and Hegel" (*Hegel's Ethics of Recognition,* 26).

79. See Shklar, "Self-Sufficient Man," 289–303, and Pöggeler, *Hegels Idee,* 263–64.

80. See Tavarès, "Hegel et l'abbé Gregoire," 155–73. The Abbe [Henri] Grégoire was surely the most loyal supporter of Haiti among the French abolitionists. In 1808, he wrote *De la littérature des Nègres,* which managed to circumvent Napoleon's censorship on the subject "ingeniously" by ostensibly dealing with the literary efforts of blacks writing in French and English: "The book was mainly about African society, but in it

has as far as I can tell been resoundingly ignored by the Hegel establishment.) But even Tavarès deals with the later Hegel, after the master-slave dialectic had been conceived.[81] No one has dared to suggest that the idea for the dialectic of lordship and bondage came to Hegel in Jena in the years 1803–5 from reading the press—journals and newspapers. And yet this selfsame Hegel, in this very Jena period during which the master-slave dialectic was first conceived, made the following notation: "Reading the newspaper in early morning is a kind of realistic morning prayer. One orients one's attitude against the world and toward God [in one case], or toward that which the world is [in the other]. The former gives the same security as the latter, in that one knows where one stands."[82]

Grégoire also took the opportunity to praise the Dominguans Toussaint Louverture and Jean Kina (who had led a revolt on Martinique) and to observe that, if Haiti was still politically unstable, this had also been true of France in the 1790s" (Geggus, "Haiti and the Abolitionists," 117). Asked in the mid-1820s to accept a bishopric in Haiti, Grégoire refused, disappointed with the conciliatory attitude of Haiti toward France when the Haitian President Boyer agreed to pay a huge indemnity to the former colonial planters in return for recognition; see Geggus, "Haiti and the Abolitionists," 128.

81. At the time of the first publication of my essay (2000), I had yet to see Tavarès' original article, "Hegel et Haiti." It deals with Hegel's Freemasonry connection. I discuss Tavarès' work in "Universal History." He raises the right questions, while his answers are based on the French sources, and remain partial and speculative. Schüller, *Die Deutsche Rezeption hatianischer Geschichte,* briefly mentions Hegel, but only his late writings (1820s), and does not suggest the direct influence I am arguing for here; nor does she suggest that Hegel read *Minerva.*

82. Rosenkranz, *Georg Wilhelm Friedrich Hegels Leben,* 543. Note that this biography is still the canonical one for Hegel, hence its republication in 1977 (and again in 1998). Although philosophical accounts of Hegel's development have been numerous and other biographies do exist, it is astonishing that Hegel has found no modern German biographer to replace Rosenkranz definitively. See, for example, Althaus, *Hegel und die heroischen Jahre der Philosophie.* Although certain objects of Hegeliana have received microscopic analysis (the watermarks on his manuscript papers, for example), there are startling gaps in our knowledge of his life. There are multiple reasons for this unevenness, beginning with the fact that Hegel moved repeatedly (from Würtemberg to Tübingen, Bern, Frankfurt, Jena, Bamberg, Nürnberg, and Heidelberg) before settling in Berlin for the last decade of his life, and he himself disposed of many documents, including personal papers, before he died. His (legitimate) son Karl was responsible for the archive after his death and may have repressed some of the sources. (Hegel's illegitimate son Ludwig, who is not mentioned in Rosenkranz's biography, was conceived in Jena in 1806 when Hegel was writing *The Phenomenology of Mind,* and died in 1831, the same year as his father, in Indonesia as a member of the Dutch merchant marines.)

We are left with only two alternatives. Either Hegel was the blindest of all the blind philosophers of freedom in Enlightenment Europe, surpassing Locke and Rousseau by far in his ability to block out reality right in front of his nose (the *print* right in front of his face at the breakfast table); or Hegel knew—knew about real slaves revolting successfully against real masters, and he elaborated his dialectic of lordship and bondage deliberately within this contemporary context.[83]

Michel-Rolph Trouillot writes in his important book *Silencing the Past* that the Haitian Revolution "entered history with the peculiar characteristic of being unthinkable even as it happened." Of course he is correct to emphasize the incapacity of most contemporaries, given their ready-made categories, "to understand the ongoing revolution on its own terms."[84] But there is a danger in conflating two silences, the past and the present one, when it comes to the Haitian story. For if men and women in the eighteenth century did not think in nonracial terms of the "fundamental equality of humanity," as "some of us do today," at least they knew what was happening; today, when the Haitian slave revolution might be more thinkable, it is more invisible, due to the construction of disciplinary discourses through which knowledge of the past has been inherited.[85]

83. *The Phenomenology of Mind* does not mention Haiti or Saint-Domingue, but it does not mention the French Revolution either, at points where the experts are in total agreement in reading the revolution into the text. Of Hegel's devotion to newspapers and journals we have abundant evidence, from his student days in Tübingen, when he followed the French revolutionary events, to the Frankfurt years in the late 1790s, when he read newspapers with pen in hand, to the 1810s and 1820s, when he recorded excerpts from the British papers, the *Edinburgh Review* and *Morning Chronicle* (see below, note 135). Immediately after finishing *The Phenomenology of Mind,* Hegel left Jena for Bamberg to become an editor of a daily newspaper himself, which foundered when Hegel was accused by the censors of disclosing the whereabouts of German troops (Hegel's defense was that he had taken this information from other, already published news sources).

84. Trouillot, *Silencing the Past,* 73.

85. Trouillot, *Silencing the Past,* 82. Trouillot discusses the various "formulas of erasure" whereby generalist histories have produced that invisibility (*Silencing the Past,* 96–98).

Eighteenth-century Europeans *were* thinking about the Haitian Revolution precisely because it challenged the racism of many of their preconceptions. One need not have been a supporter of the slave revolution to recognize its central significance to the political discourse.[86] "Even in the age of revolutions, contemporaries recognized the creation of Haiti as something extraordinary."[87] And even its opponents considered this "remarkable event" to be "worthy of the contemplation of philosophers."[88] Marcus Rainsford wrote in 1805 that the cause of the Haitian Revolution was the "spirit of liberty."[89] The fact that this spirit *could* be catching, crossing the line not only between races but between slaves and freemen, was precisely what made it possible to argue, without reverting to an abstract ontology of "nature," that the desire for freedom was truly universal, an event of *world* history and, indeed, the paradigm-breaking example. Prior to writing *The Phenomenology of Mind*, Hegel had dealt with the theme of mutual recognition in terms of *Sittlichkeit*: criminals against society or the mutual relations of religious community or personal

86. The evangelical Tory James Stephen wrote a radical pamphlet in summer 1804, arguing that white slave owners' authority rested primarily on the slaves' irrational fears, "fostered by ignorance and habit" but that, like a belief in ghosts, this "instinctive dread" once dispelled, would vanish forever (Geggus, "Haiti and the Abolitionists," 115). Henry Brougham, responding to James Stephen in the *Edinburgh Review*, "believed that the slaves' obedience derived simply from a rational calculation of the costs of resistance. . . . More free market-minded, [Brougham] thought in terms of stimulus and response" (Geggus, "Haiti and the Abolitionists," 115–16). Brougham's argument for abolishing the slave trade was also one of calculation and exigency, as the risk of rebellion had, after Haiti, increased a thousandfold; see Geggus, "Haiti and the Abolitionists," 116. We know for certain that Hegel read the *Edinburgh Review* in 1817–18, and there is speculation that his exposure to this and other British journals occurred much earlier (see note 135). Given Hegel's understanding of the modern spirit as essentially Christian, one would imagine that he would have taken Stephen's side in this debate.

87. Geggus, "Haiti and the Abolitionists," 113

88. "The French planter Drouin de Bercy thought it a remarkable event, worthy of the contemplation of philosophers and statesmen, even though he himself wished to see it destroyed and its population massacred or deported" (Geggus, "Haiti and the Abolitionists," 113).

89. See Rainsford, *Historical Account*, chap. 2.

affection. But now this young lecturer, still only in his early thirties, made the audacious move to reject these earlier versions (more acceptable to the established philosophical discourse) and to inaugurate, as the central metaphor of his work, not slavery versus some mythical state of nature (as those from Hobbes to Rousseau had done earlier), but slaves versus masters, thus bringing into his text the present, historical realities that surrounded it like invisible ink.

8

Let us consider, in more detail, Hegel's dialectic of lordship and bondage and concentrate on the salient characteristics of this relationship. (I will draw not only on the relevant passages in *The Phenomenology of Mind* but also the Jena texts that immediately preceded it, 1803–6.)[90]

90. To do justice to the variations in the Jena texts, and hence to the development of Hegel's idea of the master-slave dialectic within the historical context of the Haitian Revolution, would require an article in itself. A truly scholarly account cannot be attempted here. I can only suggest a hypothesis, one that considers Hegel's reading of Adam Smith in 1803 to be the turning point. In the first Jena *Systementwürfe* (1803–4) Hegel thematizes the "battle for recognition" in a way that marks a break from both the classical concept of ethical community (*Sittlichkeit*) and the Hobbesean concept of individual self-preservation (the state of nature). The crucial, final "fragment 22" (parts of which are crossed out and rewritten, and at least a page of which is missing) begins with a discussion of the "absolute necessity" of "mutual recognition": injury to property must be avenged "to the point of death" (Hegel, *Jenaer Systementwürfe I*, 218n2). Speaking of the property-owning head of family, Hegel writes: "if he will risk a wound, and not life itself," then "he becomes a slave of the other [*er wird der Sklav des andern*]" (*Jenaer Systementwürfe I*, 221; the German word normally is *Sklave*; note that here, and throughout his work, Hegel uses *both* terms, *Knecht* and *Sklav(e)* in the dialectic of mutual recognition). But what if the "property" is itself the injurer, the slave who rectifies the injury to *his person* by asserting his own freedom without compensation? Hegel does not raise this question but moves, rather, to a discussion of the "customs" of "the people" (*das Volk*) and the common "work" of all. This takes him in a strikingly non-Hobbesean direction, to a critique of the stunting and repetitive work of modern manufactory labor (the division of labor, exemplified by Smith's pin manufactory); see Hegel, *Jenaer Systementwürfe I*, 227–28. Hegel then critically describes the uncontrolled and "blind" interdependence of laborers in the global economy, the "bürgerliche Gesellschaft" of market exchange that forms a "monstrous system" (*ungeheueres System*) of mutual "dependency"

Hegel understands the position of the master in both political *and* economic terms. In the *System der Sittlichkeit* (1803): "The master is in possession of an overabundance of physical necessities generally, and the other [the slave] in the lack thereof."[91] At first consideration the master's situation is "independent, and its essential

---

(*Abhängigkeit*) and that "like a wild beast needs to be tamed" (*Jenaer Systementwürfe I*, 229, 230). Fragment 22 ends (in 1804!) just at the point where Hegel's discussion of "possession" (*Besitz*), as the form in which the generality of "the thing" (*das Ding*) is "recognized" (*anerkannt*), would have led him to confront the contradiction that the law of private property treats the slave (whose existence is nothing but to labor) as a thing! The slave is the one commodity like no other, as freedom of property and freedom of person are here in direct contradiction. Is it for this reason that Hegel's manuscript breaks off suddenly? The revolt of the slaves in Saint-Domingue, in this context, saved Hegel from the bad infinity (the "monstrous system") of contract reciprocity by providing the link (via a shift in emphasis from exchange to labor) from an economic system (the infinite system of needs) to politics: the founding, through a struggle unto death, of the constitutional state.

91. Hegel, *System der Sittlichkeit*, 35; quoted in Harris, "Concept of Recognition," 234; Harris comments: "The concept of legal personality emerges hand in hand with the institution of money as the 'indifference' of (i.e., the universal expression for) property. This world of formal recognition is then differentiated into masters and servants *by the extent of their possessions* (that is, ultimately in terms of money)" ("Concept of Recognition," 233).

It is the *System der Sittlichkeit* that first registers Hegel's reading of Adam Smith and also the unequal relationship of lord (*Herr*) and servant (*Knecht*) that is "established along with the inequality of the power of life" (*System der Sittlichkeit*, 34)—although these two themes do not yet come together. Hegel is concerned with the exchange of "surplus" as a "system of needs" that is "empirically unending"—that "borderless" commerce by which a people is "dissolved" (that is, returns to a "state of nature"?) (*System der Sittlichkeit*, 82, 84–85). The fact that in the exchange of private property "things have equality with other things" becomes the basis of legal right, but only through contract as the "binding middle term." It is impossible to say of life, as one can say of other things, that the individual "possesses" it; hence the connection of "lordship" [*Herrschaft*] and "bondage" [*Knechtschaft*] is one of "relationlessness" (*System der Sittlichkeit*, 32–37). Hegel notes that "among many peoples the woman is sold off by the parents—but this cannot be the basis of a marriage contract between man and wife." (But what of his own European culture where slaves are bought and sold?) "There is no contract with the bondsman [*Knecht*] either, but there can be a contract with someone else about the bondsman or the woman" (*System der Sittlichkeit*, 37). Thus "the situation of slaves [*Sklavenstand*] is not a social class (*Stand*), for it is only formally a universal. The slave [*der Sklave*] is related as a singularity [*Einzelnes*] to his master" (*System der Sittlichkeit*, 63). The lecture manuscript from which the *System der Sittlichkeit* was written up (since lost) degenerated into "mere history," according to Haym (*Hegel und seine Zeit*; quoted in Harris, "Concept of Recognition,"164); it would be interesting to know just what this "mere history" concerned.

nature is to be for itself"; whereas "the other," the slave's position, "is dependent, and its essence is life or existence for another."[92] The slave is characterized by the lack of recognition he receives. He is viewed as "a thing"; "thinghood" is the essence of slave consciousness —as it was the essence of his legal status under the *Code Noir*.[93] But as the dialectic develops, the apparent dominance of the master reverses itself with his awareness that he is in fact totally dependent on the slave. One has only to collectivize the figure of the master in order to see the descriptive pertinence of Hegel's analysis: the slaveholding class is indeed totally dependent on the institution of slavery for the "overabundance" that constitutes its wealth. This class is thus incapable of being the agent of historical progress without annihilating its own existence.[94] But then the slaves (again, collectivizing the figure) achieve self-consciousness by demonstrating that they are not things, not objects, but subjects who transform material nature.[95] Hegel's text becomes obscure and falls silent at this point of realization.[96] But given the historical events that pro-

92. Hegel, *Phenomenology of Mind*, 234.

93. Hegel, *Phenomenology of Mind*, 235

94. Historical agency then passes to the slave, who "will invent history, but only after the master has made humanity possible" (Kelly, "Hegel's 'Lordship and Bondage,'" 270).

95. The stress on labor is intriguing. The slave materializes his own subjectivity through labor. Hegel seems to privilege craft or agricultural labor (as did Adam Smith, given the dehumanizing effects of modern labor). But reading backward from Hegel's lectures on the philosophy of history (discussed below), this attitude toward labor describes the transformation within the slave's consciousness from an earlier, "African" spirit of seeing nature as itself subjectivity, to a modern spirit, wherein working on nature is an expression of one's own subjectivity.

96. The text states, "Through work and labor, however, this consciousness of the bondsman comes to itself"—positively, as the bondman's awareness "of himself as factually and objectively self-existent," and, negatively, as objectivized consciousness: "For in shaping the thing it [his consciousness] only becomes aware of its own proper negativity, its existence on its own account, as an object, through the fact that it cancels the actual form confronting it. But this objective negative element is precisely the alien, external reality, before which it trembled. Now, however, it destroys this extraneous alien negative, affirms and sets itself up as a negative in the element of permanence, and thereby becomes for itself a self-existent being" (Hegel, *Phenomenology of Mind*, 238–39). Marxists have interpreted the slave's coming to self-consciousness as a metaphor

vided the context for *The Phenomenology of Mind,* the inference is clear. Those who once acquiesced to slavery demonstrate their humanity when they are willing to risk death rather than remain subjugated.[97] The law (the *Code Noir!*) that acknowledges them merely as "a thing" can no longer be considered binding,[98] although before, according to Hegel, it was the slave himself who was responsible for his lack of freedom by initially choosing life over liberty, mere self-preservation.[99] In *The Phenomenology of Mind,* Hegel insists that freedom cannot be granted to slaves from above. The self-liberation of the slave is required through a "trial by death": "And it is solely by risking life that freedom is obtained. . . . The individual, who has not staked his life, may, no doubt, be recognized as a Person

---

for the working class's overcoming of false consciousness: the class-in-itself becomes for-itself. But they have criticized Hegel for not taking the next step to revolutionary practice. I am arguing that the slaves of Saint-Domingue were, as Hegel knew, taking that step for him.

97. I am suggesting that the arguments of several black scholars, which they believed to be *in opposition to* Hegel, are in fact close to Hegel's original intent. See, for example, Paul Gilroy, who reads Frederick Douglass (who was U.S. ambassador to Haiti in 1889) as providing an alternative to what he understands to be Hegel's "allegory" of the master and slave: "Douglass's version is quite different. For him, the slave actively prefers the possibility of death to the continuing condition of inhumanity on which plantation slavery depends" (Gilroy, *Black Atlantic,* 63). See also Orlando Patterson, who claims that the "social death" that characterized slavery required as the negation of the negation, not labor (which he sees as Hegel's meaning), but liberation, although (ultimately like Hegel) he sees this as possible through an institutional rather than revolutionary process; see Patterson, *Slavery and Social Death,* 98–101.

98. Compare Hegel's statement in 1798: "Institutions, constitutions, and laws, which no longer harmonize with the opinions of mankind and from which the spirit has departed, cannot be artificially kept alive" (quoted in Gooch, *Germany and the French Revolution,* 297). Note that Napoleon's attempt to reestablish the obsolete *Code Noir* would precisely *not* be a world-historical act; Haiti was at this moment on the side of world history, not Napoleonic France. Similarly, in the case of Germany: "Thus it was in the war with the French Republic that Germany found by its own experience that it was no longer a state" (quoted in Williams, *Hegel's Ethics of Recognition,* 346). Consciousness was only attained through a struggle of resistance against the invading French army.

99. Hegel held to this insistence on the slave's responsibility. In the *Philosophy of Right* (1821): "If a man is a slave, his own will is responsible for his slavery, just as it is its will which is responsible if a people is subjugated. Hence the wrong of slavery lies at the door not simply of enslavers or conquerors but of the slaves and the conquered themselves" (Hegel, *Philosophy of Right,* 239).

[the agenda of the abolitionists!]; but he has not attained the truth of this recognition as an independent self-consciousness."[100] The goal of *this* liberation, *out* of slavery, cannot be subjugation of the master in turn, which would be merely to repeat the master's "existential impasse,"[101] but, rather, elimination of the institution of slavery altogether.

Given the facility with which this dialectic of lordship and bondage lends itself to such a reading, one wonders why the topic Hegel and Haiti has for so long been ignored. Not only have Hegel scholars failed to answer this question; they have failed, for the past two hundred years, even to ask it.[102]

9

Surely a major reason for this omission is the Marxist appropriation of a social interpretation of Hegel's dialectic. Since the 1840s, with the early writings of Karl Marx, the struggle between the master and slave has been abstracted from literal reference and read once again as a metaphor—this time for the class struggle. In the twentieth cen-

100. Hegel, *Phenomenology of Mind*, 233.

101. This term is from Kojève, *Introduction to the Reading of Hegel*. Translator Raymond Queneau assembled notes of these lectures by Kojève and published them in French in 1947.

102. As far as I know, Tavarès is the sole exception, although many writings about African slavery have brought Hegel's master-slave dialectic to bear on their concerns. See, for example, the conclusion to Davis, *Problem of Slavery in the Age of Revolution*, 560, which suggests that we "indulge in a bit of fantasy" by interpreting Hegel's master-slave dialectic through an imagined dialogue between Napoleon and Toussaint Louverture. See the numerous accounts of W. E. B. Du Bois's writings on slavery that read these texts in relation to those of Hegel; for example, see Williamson, *The Crucible of Race*; Zamir, *Dark Voices*; and the introduction to Lewis, *W. E. B. Du Bois: A Reader*. See also Fanon, *The Wretched of the Earth*, which uses European philosophy as a weapon against European (white) hegemony, interpreting the master-slave dialectic both socially (using Marx) and psychoanalytically (using Freud) in order to theorize the necessity of violent struggle by Third World nations to overcome colonial status and to reject the hypocritical humanism of Europe, attaining equal recognition in terms of their own cultural values. Martinique-born Fanon would perhaps have been the closest to seeing the connection between Hegel and Haiti, but it was not his concern.

tury, this Hegelian-Marxist interpretation had powerful proponents, including Georg Lukács and Herbert Marcuse, as well as Alexandre Kojève, whose lectures on *The Phenomenology of Mind* were a brilliant rereading of Hegel's texts through Marxian glasses.[103] The problem is that (white) Marxists, of all readers, were the least likely to consider real slavery as significant because within their stagist understanding of history, slavery—no matter how contemporary—was seen as a premodern institution, banned from the story and relegated to the past.[104] But only if we presume that Hegel is narrating a self-contained European story, wherein "slavery" is an ancient Mediterranean institution left behind long ago, does this reading become remotely plausible—remotely, because even within Europe itself in 1806, indentured servitude and serfdom had still not disappeared, and the laws were still being contested as to whether actual slavery would be tolerated.[105]

There is an element of racism implicit in official Marxism, if only because of the notion of history as a teleological progression. It was evident when (white) Marxists resisted the Marx-inspired thesis of the Trinidad-born Eric Williams in *Capitalism and Slavery* (1944)—seconded by the Marxist historian, Trinidad-born C. L. R. James in

103. Kojève's reading of Hegel is phenomenological in a (Heideggerian) sense that sets it apart from the Marxists mentioned in the previous note because it approaches the dialectic of recognition as an existential-ontological problem, not as a logic of historical stages. Kojève connects Hegel's discussion with ancient slavery and the writings of Aristotle at the same time that he makes visible its modern form as the structure of class struggle.

104. See the works of the historian Eugene Genovese (for example, *The Political Economy of Slavery*) for a clear example of this Marxist approach to modern slavery.

105. See above, note 21, and "Universal History," 93–94. The freeing of the Prussian serfs would take place one year after the publication of *The Phenomenology of Mind*. The Danes, in 1804, were the first to end the slave trade, three years before the British. The British abolished slavery in 1831; France definitively in 1848; Russia (and the United States) not until 1861—but British abolitionists considered Tsar Alexander I an ally in convincing the Concert of Europe to discourage the French from seeking to reconquer Haiti. Thomas Clarkson met the tsar at the Congress of Aix-la-Chapelle (1818) and "showed him a letter from the King of Haiti [Henri Christophe] to impress on him the latter's abilities" (Geggus, "Haiti and the Abolitionists," 120).

The Black Jacobins—that plantation slavery was a quintessentially modern institution of capitalist exploitation.[106] As for the field of Hegel scholarship, Ludwig Siep and others have justifiably criticized the Marxist reading of Hegel in terms of the class struggle as anachronistic. But the result among philosophers has been a tendency to turn away from social contextualization completely.[107] The class-struggle interpretation of Hegel is indeed anachronistic; but that should have led interpreters to look at historical events contemporary with Hegel, not to throw out a social interpretation altogether.

Marxist-driven scholarship has, however, illuminated an entire area of Hegel's concerns that was completely underappreciated until the twentieth century. That is the fact that in 1803 Hegel read Adam Smith's *Wealth of Nations* and it led him to move to an understanding of civil society—"die bürgerliche Gesellschaft"—as modern economy, the society created by the actions of bourgeois exchange. But whereas Marxists have been excited by Hegel's citing of Smith's example of pin making in the discussion of the division of labor (which in no way fits the model of the dialectic of master and slave!)

106. The second, revised edition of James's *The Black Jacobins* (1963) specifically supports the thesis that slave existence in the colonies was "in its essence a modern life" (James, *Black Jacobins*, 392). This position has been argued as well by Du Bois: "Negro slaves in America represented the worst and lowest conditions among *modern* laborers" (Du Bois, *Black Reconstruction in America*, 9; my emphasis). When it comes to historical interpretations, however, black scholars have generally accepted the stagism of European discourse.

107. Alex Honneth is representative here when he concludes that Marx's social reading of mutual recognition in Hegel is "highly problematic" in its coupling of the romanticists' expressive anthropology (labor), the Feuerbachean concept of love, and English national economy (Honneth, *The Struggle for Recognition*, 147). Note that Ludwig Siep's interpretation stresses Hegel's move away from Hobbes with the master-slave dialectic, a reading that in fact bolsters the case that I am making here. See Siep, *Anerkennung als Prinzip der praktische Philosophie*; see also Siep's influential article "The Struggle for Recognition," 273–88. Current discussions of the master-slave dialectic (Gilles Deleuze, Jacques Derrida, and Judith Butler) confront Kojève's reading with Nietzsche's account of master and slave, thereby changing the social significance of the debate. Nietzsche criticizes as slave mentality those who submit to the state and its laws, the institutions that Hegel affirmed as the embodiment of mutual recognition, and hence concrete freedom.

they have failed to comment on the fact that Smith included an economic discussion of modern slavery in *Wealth of Nations*.[108]

It has long been recognized that Hegel's understanding of politics was modern, based on an interpretation of the events of the French Revolution as a decisive break from the past and that he is referring to the French Revolution in *The Phenomenology of Mind,* even when he does not mention it by name.[109] Why should Hegel have been a modernist in two senses only: adopting Adam Smith's theory of the economy and adopting the French Revolution as the model for politics. And, yet, when it came to slavery, the most burning social issue of his time, with slave rebellions throughout the colonies and a successful slave revolution in the wealthiest of them—why should—how *could* Hegel have stayed somehow mired in Aristotle?[110]

Beyond a doubt Hegel knew about real slaves and their revolutionary struggles. In perhaps the most political expression of his career, he used the sensational events of Haiti as the linchpin in his argument in *The Phenomenology of Spirit*.[111] The actual and successful revolution of Caribbean slaves against their masters is the moment when the dialectical logic of recognition becomes visible as the thematics of

108. See Smith, *An Inquiry*, 105–75, for discussions of colonial slavery and the slave trade and above, 4–6.

109. Experts who disagree in other ways (for example, Hyppolite, *Genesis and Structure,* and Forster, *Hegel's Idea of a Phenomenology of Spirit*) are in accord on this point. See also Riedel, *Between Tradition and Revolution*.

110. Compare Schelling's comment in a letter to Hegel dated 5 January, 1795: "Who wants to bury himself in the dust of antiquity when the movement of *his own* time at every turn sweeps him up and carries him onward?" (Hegel, *Hegel, The Letters*, 29). At the time of the French Revolution, the ancients were a discourse of the *present,* not a means of relegating the present to the past. Aristotle walked among the living as a contemporary.

111. Relevant here is the argument of Theodor Haering at the Hegel Congress in Rome in 1933, whose investigation of the coming-to-be of *The Phenomenology of Mind* led him to the "astounding" conclusion that the book is *not* organically or carefully composed according to a plan but a series of sudden decisions, pressured from within and without in an almost unimaginably short time—specifically the summer of 1806; see Pöggeler, *Hegels Idee,* 193. Haering's observations are compatible with the argument I am making here.

world history, the story of the universal realization of freedom. If the editor of *Minerva*, Archenholz, reporting history as it happened, did not himself suggest this on the pages of his journal, Hegel, long-time reader of them, was capable of that vision. Theory and reality converged at this historical moment. Or, to put it in Hegelian language, the rational—freedom—became real. This is the crucial point for understanding the originality of Hegel's argument, by which philosophy burst out of the confines of academic theory and became a commentary on the history of the world.

10

There would be much research to do. Other texts of Hegel need to be read with the Haitian connection in mind.[112] For example, the section in Hegel's *The Phenomenology of Mind* criticizing the pseudo-science of phrenology takes on a different import when it is seen as a critique of already extant theories of biological racism.[113] So does

112. The philological scrupulousness of, for example, Norbert Waszek's work on Hegel's reading of the Scottish Enlightenment philosophers provides a model, the study that illuminated Hegel's reception of Smith in a way that fundamentally changed our understanding of Hegel's philosophy of civil society; see Waszek, *Scottish Enlightenment*. We also need research not only on *Minerva* but on other German journals, and books as well, that discussed events in Saint-Domingue. See Schüller's paradigmatic work, *Die Deutsche Rezeption haitianischer Geschichte*.

113. The sections immediately following "Lordship and Bondage," those titled "Stoicism," "Scepticism," and "The Unhappy Consciousness," can be thought to refer, not to different stages of history (as Rozenkranz argued in *Hegels Leben*, 205), but rather to different modalities of thinking about the existing reality of slavery. As for the long section critiquing physiognomy and phrenology (see Hegel, *Phenomenology of Mind*, 338–72), Tavarès, who first broke the silence on Hegel and Haiti, finds it striking that commentators on Hegel "have never inscribed [this] critique . . . within the colonial debate" (Tavarès, "Hegel et l'abbé Grégoire," 168). Although the editors of both German and English editions of *The Phenomenology of Mind* do say that Hegel, while eschewing names, was referring to the work of the anatomist Franz Joseph Gall and the physiognomist Johann Kaspar Lavater, nonetheless, they make no reference to the racism inherent in these men's theories. Against Gall's comparative anatomy of crania, Hegel states, "the spirit is not a bone," and as a consequence, argues Tavarès, not about the color of skin ("Hegel et l'abbé Grégoire," 167).

Hegel's reference in *The Philosophical Propaedeutic* (1803–13) to Robinson Crusoe, which insists on coupling this prototype of man in the "state of nature"—shipwrecked on a Caribbean island—with Friday, his slave, an implicit criticism of Hobbes's individualistic version of the natural state.[114] Hegel's earliest lectures on *The Philosophy of Right* (Heidelberg, 1817–18) contain a passage that now becomes fully legible. It begins with the crucial point of the slave's *self*-liberation: "Even if I am born a slave [*Sklave*], and nourished and raised by a master, and if my parents and forefathers were all slaves, still I am free in the moment that I will it, when I become conscious of my freedom. For the personality and freedom of my will are essential parts of myself, my personality."[115]

Hegel continues: even if freedom means to have property rights, the possession of another person is excluded—"and if I have some-one whipped, it does not damage the person's freedom."[116] It is clear that Hegel is speaking here of modern slavery, and clear that con-sciousness of one's freedom demands that one *become* free, not only in thought, but *in the world*. The new version of these lectures given by Hegel his first year in Berlin (1818–19) connected the liberation of the slave explicitly with the historical realization of freedom: "That humans become free is thus part of a free world. That there be no slavery [*Sklaverei*] is the ethical requirement [*die sittliche Forderung*]. This requirement is only thereby fulfilled when what a human being ought to be appears as the external world that he makes his own."[117] We would not share the perplexity of the editor of these lectures, who noted in 1983 that Hegel "spoke surprisingly frequently of

114. Near the summary of the master-slave relation in *The Philosophical Propaedeutic,* Hegel places in parentheses: "History of Robinson Crusoe and Friday" (Hegel, *Philo-sophical Propaedeutic,* 62). See the gloss of this comment in Guietti, "A Reading of Hegel's Master/Slave Relationship," 48–60.
115. Hegel, *Die Philosophie des Rechts,* 55.
116. Hegel, *Die Philosophie des Rechts,* 228.
117. Hegel, *Die Philosophie des Rechts,* 228.

slaves."[118] And we would consider it confirmation (whereas others have hardly noticed) that Hegel in his late work *The Philosophy of Subjective Spirit* mentions the Haitian Revolution by name.[119]

It would also be revealing to revisit the argument put forth by the French philosopher Jacques d'Hont that Hegel was connected with radical Freemasonry during these years, because Freemasonry is a part of our story at every turn.[120] Not only was *Minerva*'s editor Archenholz a Mason, along with its regular correspondents, Konrad Engelbert Oelsner (whom Hegel met in 1794) and Georg Forster (whose work Hegel noted), as well as many other of Hegel's intellectual contacts;[121] not only was the English captain Rainsford a

118. Itling's editorial notes to Wannenmann's Heidelberg notes, Hegel, *Die Philosophie des Rechts*, 295n69.

119. Hegel's *The Philosophy of Subjective Spirit* (pt. 3 of the *Encyclopedia* [1830]) is a crucial document, particularly the sections "Anthropology" and "Phenomenology"; it contains consequences of Hegel's lectures on the philosophy of history, with their prejudice against African culture and more racist statements about Negroes; it also contains a fuller account of the master-slave dialectic than that found in *The Phenomenology of Mind* of 1807. Here *Sklave* and *Knecht* are still used interchangeably; here the historical trajectory is codified, with European slavery referring to the ancients; here the struggle to death is still necessary: "thus, freedom has to be *struggled* for . . . bring[ing] himself as he brings others into *peril* of *death,*" while Negroes "are sold and allow themselves to be sold without any reflection as to the rights or wrongs of it." And yet: "They cannot be said to be ineducable, for not only have they occasionally received Christianity with the greatest thankfulness . . . but in Haiti they have even formed a state on Christian principles" (Hegel, *Philosophy of Subjective Spirit,* 3:57, 3:431, 2:53, 2:55, 2:393).

120. See d'Hondt, *Hegel Secret.* This book makes the original argument that the "secret" Hegel is revealed through his connections to radical Freemasonry (while d'Hondt does not mention Saint-Domingue).

121. D'Hondt states that Archenholz belonged to the Freemasons since the 1760s; see *Hegel Secret,* 12; see also Ruof, *Johann Wilhelm von Archenholtz,* 11, and Rieger, *Johann Wilhelm von Archenholz als "Zeitbürger,"* 176. See d'Hondt, *Hegel Secret,* 23–29, for d'Hondt 's discussion of *Minerva* as a Masonic publication, which included articles from the politically radical and cosmopolitan *Chronique des mois,* "the most Girondist and the most Masonic of French thought. . . . It is the spirit of Condorcet [founder of the *Chronique*] and Brissot that are insinuated in *Minerva*" (*Hegel Secret,* 26). D'Hondt analyzes the Masonic imagery on the cover of the first issue of *Minerva,* which, he asserts, was in the hands of Hegel, Schiller, and Hölderlin in their student days (*Hegel Secret,* 8). D'Hondt lists as Freemasons in Hegel's "entourage" Georg Forster (whose writings on the French Revolution Hegel excerpted while in Bern); Konrad Engelbert Oelsner (whose meeting with Hegel in Bern [see above] might have been facilitated through Masonic connections); as well as Wieland, Körner, Sömmering, Campe, Garve, and Gleim; also Johann Samuel

Mason, author of the book on the history of Haitian independence, a translated chapter of which was published in *Minerva* in 1805,[122] but (here d'Hont's account is silent) Freemasonry was a crucial factor in the uprisings in Saint-Domingue.

It was not unusual for "mulatto" children of white colonial planters (sometimes with the mothers being legal wives) to be brought back to France and educated. And it is remarkable that the egalitarian lodges of the radical French Freemasons were a space in which racial, religious, and even sexual segregation could be at least temporarily overcome.[123] Polverel, the man who shared with Sonthonax both the post of commissioner to Saint-Domingue and responsibility for declaring the abolition of slavery within the colony in 1793, had been a Mason in Bordeaux in the 1770s,[124] a time when

---

Ersch, literary historian, friend, and collaborator of Archenholz, who was in Jena at the same time as Hegel (Archenholz contemplated moving his journal to that city in 1800, but, instead, Ersch moved to Halle; see Hegel, letter to Schelling, August 16, 1803, *Hegel, The Letters*, 66); also Johann Friedrich von Cotta, Hegel's publisher and friend from 1802 to the end of his life. D'Hondt remarks that historians of Hegel have neglected to inventory the influence of *Minerva* on Hegel because "without doubt" it displeased them; but he is impressed by "the extreme discretion of Hegel himself" regarding Freemasonry, which d'Hondt explains as necessary because of censorship and the police (*Hegel Secret*, 9).

122. See Rainsford, "Toussaint-Louverture," 276–98, 392–408. See Geggus, "British Occupation of Saint Domingue," for Rainsford's Masonic connection.

123. Local French Masonic lodges were known to include blacks, Muslims, Jews, and women, although at Bordeaux the *loge anglaise* excluded Jews and actors; see Roberts, *Mythology of the Secret Societies*, 51. Masonic "lodges throughout France were the only places where French people, whatever their rank, trade or religion, met on an equal footing animated by a spirit of unity. Instead of the old spirit of class that formerly had bound together all the noblemen of France, Freemasonry organized a good-fellowship which included all ranks and races" (Fay, *Revolution and Freemasonry*, 224).

124. Etienne de Polverel's name is connected with two lodges in Bordeaux, *L'Amitié* and *L'Harmonie sous Directoire Écossais*. Sonthonax was not a Mason (but he was a member of the Amis des Noirs). Polverel had written two days before abolition: "For a long time the African race has suffered the calumny of it being said that without slavery its members would never be accustomed to work. Let me attempt to contradict this prejudice, no less absurd than that of an aristocracy of color. . . . There will be none but brothers, Republicans, enemies of every type of tyranny—monarchy, nobility, or priesthood" (Cauna, "Polverel et Sonthonax," 51–52). This emphasis on the virtue of labor was a Masonic value, manifested in the central allegorical importance of the "Mason" craft.

a surprising number of young mulattoes who later became leaders of the revolt in Saint-Domingue were also in this seaport, slave-trading town.[125] Two of these, Vincent Ogé and Julien Raimond, educated in France as lawyers, spoke out for mulatto rights in the first year of the French Revolution. Their lack of success led them in very different directions. With the support of the Amis des Noirs and probable Masonic as well as abolitionist connections in London and Philadelphia, Ogé returned to the colony in 1790 to lead a revolt of free mulattoes for citizen rights; defeated, he was tortured and executed by the colonial court the following year.[126] Raimond was made commissioner of the colony by the French government in 1796 and worked closely first with Sonthonax and then with Toussaint, whom he helped to draft the constitution of 1801. A third Bordelais-raised mulatto, André Rigaud, fought with the French army in the American War of Independence and was, after Toussaint (who became his rival), perhaps the most important general in the Saint-Dominguan struggle against the British during the decade of the 1790s.[127] A fourth was Alexandre Pétion, who fought with Dessalines against the French, becoming president of the Haitian republic that was established in the south of the island after Dessalines's assassination in 1806. President Pétion encouraged Simón Bolivar to demand the abolition of slavery in Latin America's struggle for independence, in which Freemasonry also played a significant role. The historian de Cauna writes of this il-

125. Bordeaux in precisely these years (1802–4) briefly overtook Nantes as leader in the triangular trade of slaves and sugar. See Saugera, *Bordeaux, port négrier*.

126. Blackburn reports that Ogé, seeking to "vindicate mulatto rights before the National Assembly [in Paris], . . . returned to the colony via London, where he raised money from Clarkson and the Abolition Society. Ogé also visited the United States where he purchased arms. These travels seem to have been facilitated by Masonic connections" (Blackburn, *Overthrow of Colonial Slavery*, 182).

127. James tells us that Rigaud, "a genuine Mulatto, that is to say the son of a white and a black," was well educated at Bordeaux and learned the trade of a goldsmith. He enlisted as a volunteer in the French army that fought in the American War of Independence (James, *Black Jacobins*, 96–97).

lustrious group of Saint-Dominguan leaders: "It would be interesting to research whether they also had entered the Masonic lodges of Bordeaux. That research has yet to be done."[128] Moreover, we cannot be blind to the possibility of reciprocal influence, that the secret signs of Freemasonry were themselves affected by the ritual practices of the revolutionary slaves of Saint-Domingue. There are intriguing references to Vodou—the secret cult of Saint-Dominguan slaves that spawned the massive uprising of August 1791—as "a sort of religious and dancing masonry."[129] We know far too little of Freemasonry in the black/brown/white Atlantic, a major chapter in the history of hybridity and transculturation.

11

"The owl of *Minerva* spreads its wings only with the coming of the dusk." This often-cited statement from Hegel's lectures on *The Philosophy of History* (1822), which may well have had the journal *Minerva* in mind, in fact marks a retreat from the radical politics of *The Phenomenology of Mind*—just how much of one in regard to Hegel's position on the French Revolution has long been the subject of debate.[130]

128. Cauna, "Polverel et Sonthonax," 49. From Sonthonax's declaration: "All negroes and those of mixed blood presently in slavery are declared free to enjoy all rights attached to the title of French citizen" (Dorigny, "Léger-Félicité Sonthonax," 3).

129. Dayan, *Haiti, History, and the Gods*, 251. Dayan notes further: "[Father] Cabon suggests that blacks might well have found white 'confabulations' to have much in common with voudu: 'Somewhat before the events of the month of August 1791, one was prompted to see a sort of Freemasonry of blacks in certain manifestations of their activities'" (*Haiti, History, and the Gods*, 251). See also the historical fictional account by the Cuban novelist Alejo Carpentier, *El Siglo de las luces* (*Explosion in a Cathedral*) (1982), which includes the figure of Ogé and speaks explicitly of the Masonic connections.

130. See d'Hondt, *Hegel et les Français*. At the end of *The Philosophy of History*, Hegel could still speak of the French Revolution as "a glorious mental dawn." And yet he criticized the Terror as "the most fearful tyranny. It exercises its power without legal formalities, and the punishment it inflicts is equally simple—*Death*. This tyranny could not last; for all inclinations, all interests, reason itself revolted against this terribly consistent Liberty which in its concentrated intensity exhibited so fanatical a shape" (Hegel, *Philosophy of History*, 447, 450–51).

FIGURE 8. "A Temple erected by the Blacks to commemorate their Emancipation." Illustration for Marcus Rainsford, *An Historical Account of the Black Empire of Hayti* (1805). Line engraving by J. Barlow after the author. On Barlow's work for this book, see Honour, *From the American Revolution to World War I*, 95.

FIGURE 9. French Masonic apron, late eighteenth century.

But at least in regard to the abolition of slavery, Hegel's retreat from revolutionary radicalism was clear.[131]

Notoriously condemning African culture to prehistory and blaming the Africans themselves for New World slavery, Hegel repeated the banal and apologetic argument that slaves were better off

131. In the outline to *The Encyclopaedia of Logic* of 1830, Hegel remarked summarily that the "genuine reason why there are no longer any slaves in Christian Europe is to be sought in nothing but the principle of Christianity itself. The Christian religion is the religion of absolute freedom, and only for Christians does man count as such, man in his infinity and universality. What the slave lacks is the recognition of his personality; but the principle of personality is Universality" (Hegel, *Encyclopaedia Logic*, 240–41). He seems to mean Protestantism here (what in his lectures on the philosophy of history he calls the modern or Germanic world). Hegel was consistently critical of the hierarchical dependencies fostered by Catholicism (the "Roman" world); he could not

in the colonies than in their African homeland, where slavery was "absolute,"[132] and endorsed gradualism: "Slavery is in and for itself *injustice,* for the essence of humanity is *Freedom;* but for this man must be matured. The gradual abolition of slavery is therefore wiser and more equitable than its sudden removal."[133] This disposition, however, was not the most striking in his lectures. Rather, it was the brutal thoroughness with which he dismissed all of sub-Saharan Africa, this "land of children," of "barbarity and wildness," from any significance for world history, due to what he deemed were deficiencies of the African "spirit."[134]

Was this change simply a part of Hegel's general conservatism during the Berlin years? Or was he reacting, again, to current events?

------

have welcomed France's Concordat with the Vatican in 1801. And, indeed, he may have seen Haiti's postrevolutionary failure as in part the consequence of the Catholicism that was the official religion in both north and south: "Here it must be frankly stated, that with the Catholic Religion no rational constitution is possible"; "Napoleon could not coerce Spain into freedom any more than Philip II could force Holland into slavery" (*Philosophy of History,* 449, 453).

132. Compare with Hegel, *Die Vernunft in der Geschichte,* 225. Sibree's translation follows Karl Hegel's edition; Hoffmeister follows that of Georg Lasson. I am noting comparatively the German and English editions for reasons explained below in note 139. Hoffmeister's edition continues here: "In all African kingdoms with which Europeans have become acquainted, slavery is indigenous. . . . It is the basis of slavery in general that a person does not yet have consciousness of his freedom and thereby becomes an object, something worthless. The lesson we derive from this, and which alone interests us is that the state of nature [that is, before the establishment of a *vernünftiger Staat*] is one of injustice" (Hegel, *Die Vernunft in der Geschichte,* 225–26).

133. Hegel, *Philosophy of History,* 96, 99. Compare Hegel, *Die Vernunft in der Geschichte,* 226.

134. "In this largest part of Africa no real history can take place. There are only accidents, or surprises that follow one after another. There is no goal, no state there, that one could observe, no subjectivity, but only a series of subjects, who destroy each other" (Hegel, *Die Vernunft in der Geschichte,* 216–17). Hegel cites Herodotus, implying nothing had changed over the centuries: "In Africa all are sorcerers"; and he repeats the story of Africans as "fetish worshippers" that one finds in Charles de Brosses, the Enlightenment contemporary of Voltaire (Hegel, *Die Vernunft in der Geschichte,* 220–22; compare with Hegel, *Philosophy of History,* 94).

Haiti was once again in the news in the teens and twenties, hotly debated by abolitionists and their opponents in the British press, including in the *Edinburgh Review,* which we know for certain Hegel was then reading.[135]

In the context of continued pressure for the abolition of slavery, developments in Haiti, the "great experiment," were monitored continually, and they evoked increasing criticism even from Haiti's former supporters.[136] At issue was the alleged brutality of King Henri Christophe[137] and the island's decline in productivity under the system of free labor (here would be the proper moment for a

135. Hegel was a regular reader of the *Edinburgh Review* in 1817–19, as we know from his excerpts from this journal; see Waszek, "Hegels Exzerpte aus der 'Edinburgh Review.'" And he read the British *Morning Chronicle* in the 1820s; see Petry, "Hegel and 'The Morning Chronicle.'" Although the preserved excerpts do not deal with Haiti, it is clear that Hegel was exposed to this new stage in the Haiti debate at a time when "the liberal *Edinburgh Review* contrasted the cruel tyranny of Christophe with the virtuous, constitutional rule of Pétion" (Geggus, "Haiti and the Abolitionists," 122). Haiti was also topical in *Minerva* again, which in 1819 published in German translation large sections of General Pamphile de Lacroix's "unbiased" history of Haiti's revolution and postrevolutionary governments; see Schüller, *Die Deutsche Rezeption haitianischer Geschichte,* 256.

136. In the 1820s, "the British abolitionists became associated with [Christophe's] northern kingdom, while their French counterparts developed links with [Pétion's] republican south. . . . The division was reinforced by a number of factors: the political preferences of the French (since the only French abolitionists concerned with Haiti, Grégoire and Lafayette, were republicans); the British preference for monarchy; the cultural leanings of the mulattoes, many of whose parents had been educated in France, whereas Christophe . . . had been born in a British colony. . . . Wilberforce [the British abolitionist] professed neutrality in the matter" (Geggus, "Haiti and the Abolitionists," 122). He, however, had personal connections with Christophe, to whom he wrote, warning of the negative European press. Wilberforce told Macaulay in 1817: "Never have I worked harder than at my Haytian letters" (Geggus, "Haiti and the Abolitionists," 123); whereas Christophe "wrote temptingly of how he would like to see his countrymen converted to Protestant Christianity, abandoning a Catholicism whose priests were corrupt and whose church defended slavery. . . . Wilberforce responded by sending works on morality, Bibles in English and French, a manual of political economy and histories of the Jesuits and the Inquisition" (Geggus, "Haiti and the Abolitionists," 123–24).

137. The "thumbscrew scandal" of 1817 brought news that "a British merchant in Haiti, suspected of being an agent for the Republic, was tortured on Christophe's orders" (Geggus, "Haiti and the Abolitionists," 125).

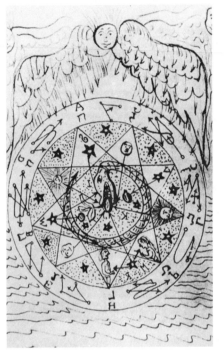

FIGURE 10. Cosmological diagram, French Freemasonry, late eighteenth century. Esoteric design by Jean-Baptiste Willermoz (Bibliothèque nationale, Paris). Willermoz, a Lyonnais businessman, was head of an Order of the Temple called Strict Observance, which had connections with Bordeaux and was strongly influenced by Martinés de Pasqually, founder of the order Élus Cohens, a mystical Masonry with the goal of reintegrating human beings to their original state before the Adamic Fall. Martinés, born in Grenoble, died in 1774 on the island of Saint-Domingue. See Hutin, *Les Francs-Maçons*, 85–90.

FIGURE 11. Cosmological diagram, Haitian Vodou, twentieth century. Ritual ground painting (*vèvè*) for the Vodou deities, assembled along a cross-shaped axis. From Desmangles, *The Faces of God*, 106. The *vèvès*, traced in powdered substances about the central column of the Vodou dancing court, "take their structure from Fon and Kongo traditions of sacred ground painting. . . . In the process, Latin Catholic attributes, the sword of St. Jacques Majeur, the hearts of the Mater Dolorosa, and *even the compass-upon-the-square of Freemasonry* have come to be interspersed along the prevailing cross-shaped axes of the majority of *vèvè* ground signs" (Thompson, "The Flash of the Spirit," 33; my emphasis).

FIGURE 12. Two-headed eagle, crowned, emblem of the Supreme Council of 33 degrees, highest order of the *rite écossais* (Scottish rite), French Freemasonry, eighteenth century (Bibliothèque nationale, Paris).

FIGURE 13. Seneque Obin, *Haitian Lodge Number 6,* 1960, depicting the two-headed eagle of the *rite écossais.* In 1801, the first Supreme Council of 33 degrees was established in Charleston, South Carolina, with both American and French brothers; one of the latter, the Count de Grassey-Tilly, "founded a new Supreme Council on the isle of Saint-Domingue" (Hutin, *Les Francs-Maçons,* 103).

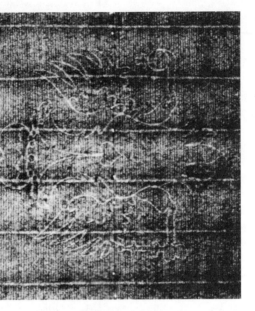

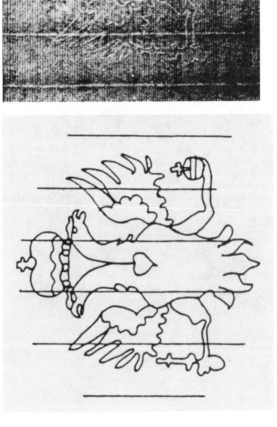

FIGURE 14 (*left*) and FIGURE 15 (*right*). Line drawing and original watermark of crowned, two-headed eagle on the paper produced by Johann Ephraim Stahl (in business from 1799, Blanckenburg an der Schwarza/Thüringen) that was used by Hegel in Jena for the last third of the manuscript of *System der Sittlichkeit* (1803). Hegel used the identical Stahl paper in September and November 1802 to record notes on politics of the day. See Ziesche and Schnitger, *Der Handschriftliche Nachlass*, 1:91–92, 2:31–32, 86.

Marxist critique).[138] We have no record as to whether these debates caused Hegel, as well, to reconsider Haiti's "great experiment." What *is* clear is that in an effort to become more erudite in African studies during the 1820s, Hegel was in fact becoming dumber.

He repeated his lectures on the philosophy of history every two years from 1822 to 1830, adding empirical material from his reading of the European experts on world history.[139] It is sadly ironic

138. Developments in Haiti were in advance of Europe in making evident the inadequacies of political equality that did not address economic inequality. The documents granting freedom to slaves in Saint-Domingue in 1794 have been criticized as being empty-handed, as they did not challenge the property rights of the large landowners, whereas the small gardens that *had* been allowed to slaves to cultivate were deemed no longer necessary: Although the ex-slaves were told, "no one has the right to require you to work a single day against your wishes," the land belonged rightly to those who inherited or bought it, so the ex-slaves needed to work, as "the only means for your supplying [your] wants is the produce of the land" (cited in Fouchard, *Haitian Maroons,* 359–60). It was in effect Sonthonax's system of land policy (maintenance of large estates where military discipline governed the laborers) that was adapted by Toussaint several years later and generalized by Dessalines's successor in the north, Christophe, whereas Polverel's unrealized proposal for distributing land to its cultivators would later be implemented in part in Pétion's republican system; see Cauna, "Polverel et Sonthonax," 52, 53. After 1823, despite President Boyer's continuation (in a united Haiti) of Christophe's policy, economic productivity was not as high as had been hoped. Boyer's *Code Rural* of 1826, while reaffirming existing smallholdings, "reduced most Haitians . . . to essentially slave status" (Dayan, *Hegel, Haiti, and the Gods,* 14). An 1827 article in the *Edinburgh Review* by Macaulay reflected "growing disillusionment" with "free labor" in Haiti because of its lack of productivity; and abolitionists generally ceased referring to the Haitian example (Geggus, "Haiti and the Abolitionists," 135, 136).

139. The first two editions of the lectures on the philosophy of history (1837 and 1840), edited by E. Gans and Karl Hegel, did not include all of the empirical material on world cultures, in what was then consequently a slim volume. Georg Lasson was the first to include comprehensively the empirical material in his three, ever more complete editions (1917, 1920, and 1930). Lasson commented in his editorial notes on the incompetence and even unscrupulousness of the earlier editors: "It is astounding how much important material was simply totally left out by the editors [Gans and Karl Hegel—the latter being the basis of the Sibree English translation]," in violation of the rigorous principles of critical philology (Hegel, *Die Vernunft in der Geschichte,* 274). Yet Lasson admits that he himself doubted whether to include all of the ethnological information that exists in Hegel's lecture notebooks, "when so much of it must appear out of date," specifically "the spiritual essence of the inhabitants of Africa" (*Die Vernunft in der Geschichte,* 277). Note that the material on Africa that appears in the Lasson (and Hoffmeister) editions is as an appendix ("Anhang: Die Alte West-Afrika"), whereas it is incorporated into the introduction in the edition of Karl Hegel (and Sibree's translation), where it is reduced from twenty-one pages to eight. The *latest* edition of Hegel's

that the more faithfully his lectures reflected Europe's conventional scholarly wisdom on African society, the less enlightened and more bigoted they became.[140]

12

Why is ending the silence on Hegel and Haiti important? Given Hegel's ultimate concession to slavery's continuance—moreover, given the fact that Hegel's philosophy of history has provided for two centuries a justification for the most complacent forms of Eurocentrism (Hegel was perhaps always a cultural racist if not a biological one)—why is it of more than arcane interest to retrieve from oblivion this fragment of history, the truth of which has managed to slip away from us?

There are many possible answers, but one is surely the potential for rescuing the idea of universal human history from the uses to which white domination has put it. If the historical facts about freedom can be ripped out of the narratives told by the victors and sal-

---

lectures on the philosophy of history (1996) includes three separate variants. The editors conclude that, for all the controversy among the editors, so long as no definitive "full" or "main" text can be ascertained, the interpretation of Hegel's philosophy of history "must remain scientifically unsatisfying" (Hegel, *Vorlesungen über die Philosophie der Weltgeschichte*, 530).

140. My conclusion here does not bear scrutiny. Rather, Hegel distorted his sources in order to fit his philosophy of history, as I discuss in "Universal History," 116–17. The master-slave dialectic becomes allegorical in Hegel's writings, a metaphor for any relation of dependency, not only the struggle to death, but just as often those that were meant to be outgrown. Some examples: In the *Encyclopedia* (1845), the subjection of the servant is "a necessary moment in the education (*Bildung*) of every man. . . . No man can, without this will-breaking discipline, become free and worthy to command"; on nations: "Bondage and tyranny are necessary things in the history of peoples"; from *The Philosophy of Religion:* "I am not one of the fighters locked in the battle, but both, and I am the struggle itself. I am fire and water" (Kelly, "Hegel's 'Lordship and Bondage,'" 271). It is in the 1825 summer semester on the phenomenology of spirit that we have a version of master and servant stressing as the good aspect of being a servant the moment of freedom in work itself; see Noerr, *Sinnlichkeit und Herrschaft*, 46–47.

vaged for our own time, then the project of universal freedom does not need to be discarded but, rather, redeemed and reconstituted on a different basis. Hegel's moment of clarity of thought would need to be juxtaposed to that of others at the time: Toussaint-Louverture, Wordsworth, the Abbé Grégoire, even Dessalines. For all his brutality and revenge against whites, Dessalines saw the realities of European racism most clearly. Even more, Hegel's moment would need to be juxtaposed to the moments of clarity in action: the French soldiers sent by Napoleon to the colony who, upon hearing these former slaves singing the "Marseillaise," wondered aloud if they were not fighting on the wrong side; the Polish regiment under Leclerc's command who disobeyed orders and refused to drown six hundred captured Saint-Domiguans.[141] There are many examples of such clarity, and they belong to no side, no one group exclusively. What if every time that the consciousness of individuals surpassed the confines of present constellations of power in perceiving the concrete meaning of freedom, *this* were valued as a moment, however transitory, of the realization of absolute spirit? What other silences would need to be broken? What *undisciplined* stories would be told?

141. See James, *Black Jacobins*, 318. Dessalines, in gratitude, and in acknowledgment of what the Poles suffered at home (he referred to them aptly as "the white negroes of Europe," as Polish serfdom was not distinguishable from slavery), allowed them to stay in Haiti after independence (whereas all other whites were barred by Article 12 of the 1805 constitution from owning property; see Dayan, *Hegel, Haiti, and the Gods*, 24; Dayan notes that some Germans and white women married to blacks were also allowed to stay). Pachonski and Wilson report that "freemasonry had numerous adherents in the 114th [Polish] Demibrigade and was at the same time . . . well rooted among San Domingo's population" (Pachonski and Wilson, *Poland's Caribbean Tragedy*, 309; see also 138, 283).

Universal History

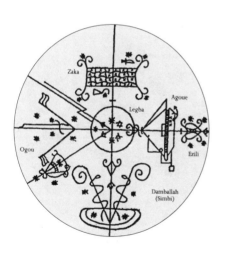

INTRODUCTION
TO PART TWO

First Remarks

TODAY'S NEOLIBERAL HEGEMONY sets the stage for "Universal History" that continues in the spirit of "Hegel and Haiti" to un-earth certain repressions surrounding the historical origins of modernity. Present realities demand such historical remappings as an alternative to the fantasies of clashing civilizations and exclusion-ary redemptions. The essay works through the historical specificities of particular experiences, approaching the universal not by sub-suming facts within overarching systems or homogenizing premises, but by attending to the edges of systems, the limits of premises, the boundaries of our historical imagination in order to trespass, trou-ble, and tear these boundaries down. The task is to reconfigure the enlightenment project of universal history in the context of our too-soon and not-yet global public sphere. It may be described as a new humanism, but if so, then without the ideological implica-tions that the suffix, -ism, usually implies. The argument is simply that with global challenges on every level, from the most material to the most moral, universal history matters.

Three Images

What happens when, in the spirit of dialectics, we turn the tables, and consider Haiti not as the victim of Europe, but as an agent in Europe's construction? The question can be approached in the form of a rebus, a picture puzzle, composed of three images.

The first is from Voltaire's *Candide*, part of a series of illustrations by the artist Jean-Michel Moreau le Jeune, that accompanied the appearance of the first *Oeuvres complètes de Voltaire* in 1787.[1] One of four scenes Moreau chose to illustrate from *Candide*, it shows the hero's encounter in the Dutch colony of Surinam with a slave who has been physically mutilated by his master. The slave explains, "[I]t is the custom. . . . When we work in the sugar mills and we catch our finger in the millstone, they cut off our hand; when we try to run away, they cut off a leg." The caption of Moreau's illustration consists of the slave's concluding words: "It is at this price that you eat sugar in Europe."[2]

When Moreau designed a second set of prints for the 1803 edition, he omitted this scene completely. Mary Bellhouse makes a convincing case that, while in Voltaire's *Candide* (first published in 1759) Dutch Surinam is a displacement for the French colony of sugar-rich Saint-Domingue, the slave revolution on that island is the source of the illustrator's later omission. She traces the generally changed nature of French visual culture with the outbreak of the Haitian revolution, from depictions of blacks as "infantilized, subservient, and dismembered" to their portrayal as physically violent and dangerously sexualized actors, reducing whites to "bodies

---

1. The image is a focus of investigation in the carefully researched article by Bellhouse, "Candide Shoots the Monkey Lovers," 741–84.
2. Bellhouse, "Candide Shoots the Monkey Lovers," 758.

FIGURE 16. Jean-Michel Moreau le Jeune, Illustration for
Voltaire's *Candide*, 1787.

in pieces," a psychic threat to emasculate European white males.[3] Applying psychoanalytic logic as the interpretive tool, she analyzes Moreau's early image in nuanced detail, discovering the "multiple signifiers of 'phallic' power" in the hands of the whites (Candide's walking stick, rifle, legs), in contrast with the mutilated slave in shadows, whose "dark skin color is linked to dismemberment."[4]

What justifies resisting such an approach to this particular image? Surely it is not for a lack of appreciation of Freud, whose hermeneutic methods have long proved theoretically productive. But there is something lost when the theoretical apparatus of psychoanalysis is mapped directly onto a political analysis of the collective unconscious, lost to both sides of the interpretive process, the personal (psychological) *and* the political (social). Granted, Bellhouse recognizes that the images elude "one stable reading."[5] And it would be churlish to reject an affective reading altogether by reducing interpretation to the simple fact that if Moreau *had* repeated his earlier illustration, it would not have passed the French censors in 1803; or to counter that James Barlow's illustrations for Marcus Rainsford's history of Haiti (1805) depicted freed slaves as classic and calm revolutionary heroes; or to note that the Paris mob was described as socially and sexually out of control even though it was overwhelmingly white. Still, if there *is* anxiety expressed in the image of the mutilated slave, we ought not to exclude consideration that it was lodged in the reality of the social situation, which cannot be reduced to the castration fears of men.[6]

3. "The long tradition in French visual culture of representing the black man as infantilized, subservient, and dismembered was upset by the eruption of massive violence in Saint-Domingue in August 1791, a date that marks the beginning of the Haitian Revolution and the beginning of a rupture in the French racialized regime of visual signification" (Bellhouse, "Candide Shoots the Monkey Lovers," 760).

4. Bellhouse, "Candide Shoots the Monkey Lovers," 758.

5. Bellhouse, "Candide Shoots the Monkey Lovers," 767.

6. I am aware that for Lacanian theorists, the penis is not the phallus, and all psychic meanings are socially mediated. That itself is not the problem. Rather, by tipping the focus of analysis toward the psychological, one loses the dialectical tension of the

In Moreau's image, political and economic impotence converge. Slavery's existence as a profitable institution, manifestly visible in the slave who has lost both leg *and* hand, was itself frightening to Europeans, and it made a difference where one stood in the socioeconomic hierarchy as to what that fear entailed.[7] Not all guilt is sexual in origin. The figure of Candide expresses the undeniable political experience of guilt that we humans feel when witnessing something deeply wrong with the principles that govern our everyday world. Something in the official order—evident but not acknowledged, spoken about but not known—contradicts its own sense of moral right. But because the authorities who speak for the whole tolerate, practice, and benefit from it, this order continues. The truth, available to conscious perception, is at the same time "disavowed," to use Sibylle Fischer's felicitous term, and moral imagination finds itself in conflict with social obedience.[8] Political guilt has its own ambivalence, because refusing to do your socially prescribed duty in order to do right entails being a traitor to the collective that claims you (through nation or class, religion or race) and risking the loss of the collective's protection as a consequence.

---

critique, the argument that psychic "health" paradoxically demands adapting to an unhealthy social reality.

7. To see fear of castration as the source of European racism, propelled by rumors of atrocities committed by rebelling colonial slaves, and to read that fear in the visual stereotypes in the "atrocity prints" of physically threatening, sexualized black males, is to short-circuit precisely the historical specificity that Bellhouse's research so brilliantly discloses. In adopting the pre-Oedipal, Lacanian language of desire and loss (the maimed slave figures as Lacan's "body in pieces"), she is led to ahistoricity against her intent: "According to psychoanalytic theory, the male is necessarily threatened with feeling inadequate in relation to other men, because the production of the masculine rests on comparison with an unknown foreclosed imago. It is for this reason that the structure of hierarchy has such a deep purchase on male subjectivity" (Bellhouse, "Candide Shoots the Monkey Lovers," 767). Where is differentiation of reception here?

8. Fischer, *Modernity Disavowed*. It is troubling how effective official disavowal can be despite the existence of democratic institutions. The U.S. government has engaged in continuous disavowal to wage its War on Terror, disavowing known facts, for which the country as a whole is then responsible. It takes a social movement to challenge such disavowal.

This is what I had in mind with the example of the French soldiers in Saint-Domingue who, hearing the officially named enemy, the self-liberating slaves singing the French revolutionary anthem, questioned whether they were not fighting on the wrong side; or the Polish regiment who refused to drown their Saint-Dominguan captives and were later acknowledged as citizens of "Black Haiti" by a grateful Dessalines.[9] The moral universality to which such actions appeal is in the register of the negative—the conditions are *not* right when judged by the official values themselves—rather than imposing one's own morality on others.[10] Such guilt has its source in the gap between reality and social fantasy, rather than between reality and individual fantasy. It can turn interpretive analysis into political critique by breaking the official silence that sanctions the wrong state of things.

We do not need Lacanian theory to interpret, as a second rebus, Spinoza's waking vision in 1664, reported by letter to his friend, a Dutch merchant, "of a certain black and mangy Brazilian, whom I had never seen before."[11] Spinoza was a persistent critic of the atomistic individualism of his contemporary, Hobbes, and insisted on the interrelatedness of human beings, anticipating Hegel by more than a century. As a philosopher, he championed the rights of the physically empowered "multitude," and yet like later Enlightenment

9. See above, "Hegel and Haiti," 75.

10. This is not an extension of the European narrative's claim on universality, but precisely the critical exposure of the untruth of that claim.

11. "When one morning just at dawn I awoke from a very deep sleep, images which came to me during sleep were as vivid to my eyes as if they had been real, in particular the image of a certain black and mangy Brazilian . . . whom I had never seen before. The image disappeared for the most part when, as a diversion, I fixed my eyes on a book or something else; but as soon as I turned my eyes away from such an object while looking at nothing in particular, the same image of the same Ethiopian kept appearing with the same vividness again and again until it gradually disappeared from sight" (cited in Montag, *Bodies, Masses, Power*, 87). Montag observes, "Spinoza's work from beginning to end remains haunted by figures of the inassimilable, the exceptions to the democracy without exceptions, and simultaneously by the impossibility of their exclusion" (*Bodies, Masses, Power*, 86).

thinkers, he closed his eyes to the social exclusions with which the multitude was riddled. "Who is this Brazilian," Warren Montag asks, "if not a condensation of all those whom Spinoza would legally deny a voice . . . [who] taken together comprise a numerical majority in any given society: women, slaves, wage labourers, foreigners? They are the multitude whose real power no laws, no constitutions can make disappear and whose very existence political philosophy seeks precisely in its most liberal forms actively to deny."[12]

The critical writing of history is a continuous struggle to liberate the past from within the unconscious of a collective that forgets the conditions of its own existence. These conditions are brought back to us in Voltaire's slave, whose missing hand stands in for Hegel's description of the division of labor's effects, the intensified tempo and dulling repetition that dismembers the mind and the body, so that the social and the psychological are inextricably interrelated. The associative link is in Hegel's choice of words for the modern labor process: *"Abstumpfung"* ("stunting," "dulling," "truncating"), translated into English as "emasculation."[13]

A final image, a third rebus, is appropriate. Adam Smith, who died on the eve of the Paris and Saint-Domingue revolutions, wrote that the work of slaves was dearer to their masters than that of freemen, and he condemned slavery as an intolerable obstacle to human progress. Yet he was fully aware of the enormous profits of the sugar plantations—particularly in Barbados and Saint-Domingue— despite the fact that all the work was done by slaves. Was it not, then, a case of disavowal that Smith's only weakness was consuming lumps of sugar? An eyewitness recalls:

12. Montag, *Bodies, Masses, Power*, 87. Montag speculates on the basis of the Brazilian connection that Spinoza, a Jew excommunicated for heresy, felt an affinity with the mangy slave, an awareness that as outcasts they are "'objective allies' in a common struggle" (*Bodies, Masses, Power*, 88).

13. This is Avineri's translation of *Abstumpfung* (Avineri, *Hegel's Theory of the Modern State*, 94).

We shall never forget one particular evening when [Adam Smith] put an elderly maiden lady who presided at the tea-table to sore confusion by neglecting utterly her invitation to be seated, and walking round and round the circle, stopping ever and anon to steal a lump from the sugar basin, which the venerable spinster was at length constrained to place on her own knee, as the only method of securing it from his uneconomical depredations. His appearance mumping the eternal sugar was something indescribable.[14]

14. Cited in Rae, *Life of Adam Smith*, 338. "It is probably the same story Robert Chambers gives in his *Traditions of Edinburgh*, and he makes the scene Smith's own parlour, and the elderly spinster his cousin, Miss Jean Douglas" (*Life of Adam Smith*, 338). Was the lump-sugar compulsion a displacement of Smith's sexual desire for his cousin, who might have been considered "elderly" at a relatively young age, and whose own ambivalence was signaled by placing the sugar basin on her lap? Insistence on the dialectical interrelationship of the personal and the political would then necessitate the question: how did the woman as object of (illicit) sexual desire become associated with sugar in the first place?

UNIVERSAL
HISTORY

1. *Haiti and the Creation of Europe*

Slavery in Europe

COULD SLAVERY HAVE taken root in the colonizing metropoles of
Europe? The answer to this question was contested rather than as-
sured. What made colonial slavery modern was its capitalist form,
extracting maximum value by exhausting both land and labor to fill
an insatiable consumer demand created by the addictive products
themselves (tobacco, sugar, coffee, rum). Forged out of the most cur-
rent economic forces, why would the plantation system *not* become the
dominant form of industrial labor in Europe as well as the colonies?
The fact that today we find it difficult to imagine a Manchester tex-
tile revolution powered by the labor of African, Irish, and English
slaves, or a form of capitalism *not* synonymous with "free" làbor, or
economic modernization as anything but the invention of the (white)
nations of the West, attests to the effective limits placed on our his-
torical imaginations by the boundary concepts of race, nation, and

modern progress that were constructed in large part to close off these possible alternatives.

"There is no inherent reason that slavery should be incompatible with the ideal of a functional or utilitarian state," writes David Brion Davis, as he describes for the British case the interconnections among Caribbean slavery, the abolitionist movement, capitalist class interests, and the ambiguous triumph of free labor, stressing the contingency of these elements' historical coalescence.[1] Enslavement of Europeans was far from a shocking idea in the seventeenth and early eighteenth centuries when, as a workforce, the primary issue in evaluating slavery was maintaining social order rather than maximizing profits. Domestic slavery was endorsed by Thomas Hobbes, John Locke, and Samuel Pufendorf as a salutary solution to the problem of providing social discipline for the growing numbers of so-called "masterless men"—idlers, criminals, vagabonds, and paupers.[2] Penal slave labor was common.[3] Indentured servitude was an

---

1. Davis, *Problem of Slavery in the Age of Revolution,* 263.

2. "For Thomas Hobbes, slavery was an inevitable part of the logic of power; the bondsman had no cause for complaint when he was provided with sustenance and security in exchange for being governed. Samuel Pufendorf agreed . . . that slavery was therefore a highly useful instrument of social discipline, which might solve the problem of Europe's idlers, thieves, and vagabonds. John Locke recommended compulsory labor for England's landless poor, and especially for their small children who needed to be 'inured to work.' Francis Hutcheson, one of the prime sources of antislavery thought, also argued that nothing was so 'effectual' as perpetual bondage in promoting industry and restraining sloth, especially in the 'lower conditions of society.' He therefore argued that slavery should be the 'ordinary punishment of such idle vagrants as after proper admonitions and tryals [*sic.*] of temporary servitude, cannot be engaged to support themselves and their families by any useful labours'" (Davis, *Problem of Slavery,* 263–64).

3. "It is almost universally believed by European and American writers and readers of history that slavery was abolished in the northern part of Western Europe by the late Middle Ages. Yet in France, Spain, England and the Netherlands, a severe form of enslavement of Europeans by Europeans was to develop and flourish from the middle of the fifteenth century to well into the nineteenth. This was penal slavery, beginning with galley slavery and continuing with . . . penal slavery in public works" (Patterson, *Slavery and Social Death,* 44). Recently in the United States, penal slave labor has been proposed as an alternative to illegal immigrant labor for use in private enterprise.

established means of supplying workers for the colonies, their bodies sold and their labor exploited with the same callousness and cruelty as slaves.

But the mid-eighteenth century saw a quite sudden shift: "[B]y the 1760s, even the most ardent proponents of social utility refrained from recommending *slavery* as the most suitable condition for England's poor."[4] The reason for increasing misgivings was an awareness of the reality of New World slavery, as the slave population in the colonies mushroomed and production boomed. Because the cruelty of the system was not only appalling but at the same time clearly effective as a technique of labor discipline, its implications could not be ignored. The slave labor system on the New World plantations bore "a surface resemblance, to say the least," to the experiments of British industrialists, and the innovations of production described by Adam Smith.[5] Although later historians would argue that capitalist modernization was incompatible with the inefficiencies of slave labor, the issue then and, in fact, always, is not only how to exploit labor most efficiently, but how to compel the laborers to comply.

In a clear case of disavowal, the greater the volume of African slavery, and consequently the more porous (hence fictional) the boundary between slave-holding colonies and slave-rejecting Europe became, the more stringent were the laws passed in an attempt to reinforce it. The more frequent the incidences of slave-initiated revolts in the colonies that proved their desire for freedom, the more receptive Europeans were to theories of Negroes as naturally

4. Davis, *Problem of Slavery*, 264

5. Davis, *Problem of Slavery*, 459. "While English society increasingly condemned the institution of slavery, it approved experiments in labor discipline which appeared to gravitate toward the plantation model. . . . Slaveholders and industrialists shared a growing interest not only in surveillance and control but in modifying the character and habits of their workers" (*Problem of Slavery*, 458).

destined to slavery.[6] "Slavery was not born of racism; rather, racism was the consequence of slavery," wrote Eric Williams in 1944, and recent scholarship confirms it.[7] Europeans built conceptual barriers of difference in the form of spatial distinctions between nation and colonies, a racialized distinction of *Negro* slavery, and legal distinctions as to the protection of persons, in order to segregate free Europe from colonial practices. Court cases are especially revealing, as African slaves within Europe made use of principles of ancient liberty to challenge the very legality of their enslavement, testing the customary belief in both France and England that freedom was guaranteed to anyone who set foot on either country's soil. The particulars of the cases were different, but the conclusion was the same: love of liberty would require discrimination on the basis of race. Slave and Negro (*nègre*) began to appear in the discourse as synonymous.

In France, the courts had long recognized a geographic division in the Liberty principle, acknowledging the *Code Noir* of 1685 as "necessary and authorized" for the colonies.[8] But French soil in Europe was claimed to be distinct and sacred ground. A royal edict of 1716 that allowed limited residence of slaves in the company of their masters was routinely ignored by the *parlements*, which granted freedom to hundreds of slaves on the race-blind ground that slavery was illegal in France *tout court*. When the number of Africans within France was still relatively small, such magnanimity, while carrying little cost, was in accord with the nation's idea of itself.

---

6. Tackey's Revolt in Jamaica (1760) was the first of a series of such revolts that proved precisely the opposite: "Major plots and revolts subsequently erupted in Bermuda and Nevis (1761), Suriname (1762, 1763, 1768–72), Jamaica (1765, 1766, 1776), British Honduras (1765, 1768, 1773), Grenada (1765), Montserrat (1768), St. Vincent (1769–73), Tobago (1770, 1771, 1774), St. Croix and St. Thomas (1770 and after), and St. Kitts (1778)" (Linebaugh and Rediker, *Many-Headed Hydra*, 224). In the 1760s and 1770s, there were also multiple reverberations on the North American continent.

7. Williams, *Capitalism & Slavery*, 7.

8. Peabody, *"No Slaves in France,"* 36.

Elimination of slavery as an institution was not the motivation.[9] "The intent of bestowing freedom on those who traveled to France was to prevent slavery from entering the metropolis, not to increase the numbers of freedmen in the colonies," writes Sue Peabody, whose work traces a shift during the eighteenth century as the category of race appeared in legal discourse, and the principle that "there are no slaves in France" began to be interpreted in a way that made African blacks an exception.[10]

The emergence of racial distinctions guaranteed the property rights of masters, while policing the boundary between slaves and liberty. The landmark case was *Francisque v. Brignon* (1759), won by proving that Francisque, born in India, was not a *nègre* despite his dark skin, hence the principle of Liberty applied.[11] In 1777, a series of decrees known as the *Police des Noirs* prohibited the immigration of Negroes and mulattoes, whether slave or free, and attempted to prevent social and sexual integration that would blur racial distinctions on which the Liberty principle now depended.[12]

9. Peabody refers to "what was essentially a mythical relationship between France and freedom" (*"No Slaves in France,"* 39).

10. "French championship of the abstract notion of freedom coupled with the persistent, indeed expanding, reality of slavery in the colonies necessitated a justification whereby the enslavement of some peoples and not others could be explained. . . . That rationale proved, in the short run, to be racism" (Peabody, *"No Slaves in France,"* 68–69).

11. Francisque's lawyers argued: "'It is true that his nose is a bit large, his lips a little fat. But, disregarding his color, he looks more European than many Europeans who need only black skin to appear African.' . . . the lawyers linked African features to their servitude: 'by their ignoble appearance (*figure ignoble*), the negroes of Africa seem to be more especially destined to slavery'" (Peabody, *"No Slaves in France,"* 65–66).

12. The government attempted to prohibit intermarriage in France between races, regardless of the status of the Negro, slave or free. Poncet de la Grave, charged by the king with implementing the *Police des Noirs*, linked Africans with the spread of venereal disease: "contamination" as a consequence of the sexual mingling of the races. Although these decrees were eroded during the revolution, Napoleon reinstated them in 1802 (Peabody, *"No Slaves in France,"* 124–25). Miscegenation was a fear in England as well—specifically of black freemen in the metropolis. Sergeant Davy, defending Somerset in his case for freedom, nonetheless wished to prevent the influx of Negroes in England:

In England, the pivotal legal battle was in 1772, when the Court ruled in favor of the slave James Somerset, whose counsel, Sergeant Davy, argued famously, "England was too pure an Air for Slaves to breathe in"—a myth, no more historically accurate than the French claim that "there are no slaves in France"[13]—and the motivation was similar: "[Davy] made it clear that the air of England was also too pure for a Negro to breathe in. He wished to prevent the influx of Negroes."[14] The Somerset case defined slavery as essentially "un-British," an "alien intrusion" which could be tolerated at best, as an unfortunate part of the commercial and colonial "other-world."[15] Striking is the fact that the decision rested on acknowledging colonial slavery as new, "an innovation unknown to common law and 'totally different' from ancient villeinage."[16] As such, it was not protected by England's ancient liberties, and Parliament was free to regulate it by positive law, as it was already regulating the slave trade and colonial governance. For all the self-congratulatory moral righteousness that greeted the British decision in the Somerset case, "English courts endorsed no principles that undermined colonial slave law."[17]

"'for now we have some Accidents of Children born of an Odd Colour.' Unless a law were passed to prevent such immigration, Davy said, 'I don't know what our Progeny may be, I mean of what Colour.'" (Davis, *Problem of Slavery*, 495).

13. See Peabody, *No Slaves in France*.

14. Davis, *Problem of Slavery*, 495. "Somerset's counsel emphasized the danger of augmenting the existing and free-floating population of some 14,000 to 15,000 blacks who were termed 'foreign superfluous inhabitants . . . a nation of enemies in the heart of the state.' . . . By the 1770s there was a growing fear of the abandoned and unemployed blacks in London" (*Problem of Slavery*, 495).

15. Simultaneously, "increasing numbers of English women and children were being pushed into mines, mills, and workhouses, where dehumanizing labor, physical punishment, sexual exploitation, and division of families approximated the 'un-English' evils that abolitionists selected as their prime targets of attack" (Davis, *Problem of Slavery*, 402).

16. Davis, *Problem of Slavery*, 376.

17. Davis, *Problem of Slavery*, 501.

Were there slave laborers employed illegally in Europe? The fact that substantive documentation is lacking does not surprise us, as that is what an illegal immigrant labor force is all about. There is ample evidence that legal decisions were not evenly applied across the nation; juridical decentralization was the rule, and port cities were likely to be most lax in antislavery enforcement. The law itself provides evidence for the existence of European slave labor by what it deemed necessary to prohibit. Davis notes, "in 1773 Portugal forbade the entry of Brazilian slaves or free blacks, who were said to constitute unfair competition to domestic labor."[18] In rhetoric that seems more performative than descriptive, a British court case in 1771 acknowledged the unfortunate need for slavery in America: "But the slavery of negroes is unnecessary in England."[19] A letter by the German poet Klopstock is intriguing, praising the Danish king as being "the first among all the European powers to declare that humans no longer be handled as commodities (*Waare*)," and that the Danes should no longer use Negro slaves for agricultural labor (*Feldarbeit*)." [20] The Danish king's prohibition as described by Klopstock was universal regarding the handling of "humans" as commodities (Denmark was the first European country to abolish the slave trade[21]), unlike the court cases we have been describing, it

18. Davis, *Problem of Slavery*, 495.

19. Cited in Davis, *Problem of Slavery*, 488.

20. "Der König von Dännemark . . . der zuerst unter allen europäischen Mächten befohlen hat, dass die Menschen nicht länger wie Waare betrachtet werden, und die Dänen nicht mehr zu ihrer Feldarbeit Neger-Sklaven brauchen sollten" (cited in Saine, *Black Bread–White Bread,* 277). Was Klopstock referring to the 25 March 1791 Danish Ordinance for the Good Order of Serfs? Denmark's considerable reforms made a clear distinction between labor in Danish agriculture and the hot climate production of the Caribbean plantations. Klopstock received financial support from the Danish aristocrat Ernst Schimmelmann, a progressive reformer who inherited a fortune built in part from colonial slave production, and in part from serf-produced agriculture in Denmark. His wife held a salon at their summer residence north of Copenhagen.

21. On 16 March 1792, Frederik VI as Regent issued an edict to abolish the slave trade that came into effect on 1 January 1803. The King was less racist than many of

opposed making African slave labor an exception, and, given the fact that the Danes did not prohibit slave labor in the fields of their colonies until 1848, the "agricultural labor" to which Klopstock refers would appear to have been in Denmark itself. Klopstock's letter, published in *Minerva* in January 1793, was written after the self-liberation of the slaves of Saint-Domingue. Within a decade, the very success of the Haitian Revolution intensified racism as a means of segregating Europe from the impact of global events. But the story is not one-sided.

Incomplete Revolution

Toussaint Loverture's constitution of 1801, without a doubt, took universal history to the farthest point of progress by extending the principle of Liberty to all residents regardless of race, including political refugees who sought asylum from slavery elsewhere, compelling the French Jacobins (at least temporarily) to follow their lead.[22] This end to the condition of slavery cannot be overestimated. The license for torture and physical brutality of all kinds was now

---

his subjects, and led the movement for reform. In 1802, a legal appeal by the slave Hans Jonathan, to decide "whether his presence in Denmark automatically made him free," was decided against the plaintiff: "The irony was that, the Somerset case of 30 years notwithstanding and the suspension of the Danish transatlantic trade in the very same year that the case came before the court, it answered the question in the negative" (Hall, *Slave Society*, 35). Hall records the Danish Ordinance I mention in the preceding note, but he does not clarify its contents, or address the question of black slave labor within Denmark (*Slave Society*, 36).

22. Louverture's 1801 Constitution for Saint-Domingue (still the colony of France) states unequivocally: "slaves may not exist in this territory, servitude is forever abolished. Here all men are born, live, and die free and French." And further: "All men, whatever their color, are here admissible to all employments" (cited in Fischer, *Modernity Disavowed*, 263, 266). Fischer is correct to conclude that while the French Declaration of Rights as "universal" was in fact limited to French citizens, the territorially limited guarantee of rights in the Saint-Domingue constitution were more universal in their applicability, literally, to any person who entered its territory (Fischer, *Modernity Disavowed*, 266).

denied. Legal status mattered. But the Haitian experience taught Europe a very different lesson as well, that free labor need not be undisciplined labor, nor did the constitutional elimination of racial segregation prevent the sustaining of social hierarchies of skin color and class, as mulatto superiority and state-bestowed privilege became permanent features of Haitian society.[23] Neither Louverture nor Dessalines desired anything but the continuation of the plantation labor system, now employing freemen as wage laborers, but still geared toward maximum production for export.[24] The model was military discipline that had already demonstrated its capacity to organize the slave insurgents. Dubois writes, "the figure of the male slave-turned-soldier was crucial for the shaping of emancipation in the French Caribbean, where military service would be the realm in which freedom was most accessible to ex-slaves."[25] While this allowed for some social mobility regardless of background, it also provided the ideological legitimation for continued labor exploitation on the

23. Fischer cites Trouillot's description of the contradiction: "the Haitian state and the Haitian nation were launched in opposite directions"; she comments: "Whereas the nation congealed around notions of liberty from slavery, the state in fact inherited the social and economic institutions from colonial times, which required a regimented labor force" (*Modernity Disavowed*, 269).

24. Under Title VI of Toussaint's constitution of 1801: "the colony being essentially agricultural, it cannot suffer the smallest disruption in the operation of its plantations . . . each one of which is a 'manufacture' which requires the joining together of the planters and the workers." This was the beginning of "agrarian militarism," a system of regimented labor that with Dessalines's constitution remained basically intact (see Fischer, *Modernity Disavowed*, 266–67). Toussaint's foreign policy adopted the revolutionary internationalism of the Girondin. Both he and Dessalines invaded neighboring Santo Domingo in order to free the slaves, an act of revolutionary internationalism that paralleled the foreign policy of the Girondin, and Napoleon himself. Toussaint had plans to turn the western part of Santo Domingo (where small independent farmers predominated) into plantations, with disciplined labor forces, according to the agrarian militarist model.

25. Dubois, *A Colony of Citizens*, 162. For a discussion of the "profound cleavage" between "the policies, the economic orientation, and philosophy" of Toussaint and the peasants of Saint-Domingue, see Fick, *Making of Haiti*, 209, 213, 222, 237–50. At the end of Toussaint's regime, "general emancipation had, in many ways, become little more than a political abstraction with no meaningful substance in the daily lives of the greater mass of black laborers" (*The Making of Haiti*, 222).

plantations, a system that came to be called "agrarian militarism" (*caporalisme agraire*).[26] In the Americas, social stratification became integrated into the ideology of colonial independence.[27] So history is not only about Haiti's virtue and Europe's sin. There is a "darker side" within both experiences of modernity.[28]

In the Age of Revolution, liberty and equality were nowhere without qualification. British antislavery activists followed labor developments in Toussaint's regime closely, as worker discipline was uppermost in their minds. "The reformers feared, above all else, the kind of uncontrolled behavior they already associated with unruly whites—the very class of 'idle vagrants' that liberals [before the mid-1700s] . . . had wanted to have enslaved."[29] Davis discerns in British antislavery writings "an almost obsessive concern with idealizing hierarchical order," describing one of their number, the Reverend James Ramsay, as making "no attempt to disguise his ad-

26. "The attempt to control the population of plantation laborers in Saint-Domingue constituted a continual concern for the administrators who succeeded Sonthonax, notably Toussaint Louverture himself. In the late 1790s, Toussaint Louverture was particularly concerned with rebuilding the plantation economy in order to produce commodities for export, notably as a way of purchasing provisions for the colony and weapons and ammunition for his army. In this context, he perfected the system, based on the policies of Sonthonax and similar to that of Hugues in Guadeloupe, which required plantation laborers to continue working on the plantations" (Dubois, "Inscribing Race," 103).

27. The hierarchies of social privilege included Creole v. African-born, mulatto v. black, slave-background v. free, landholder v. plantation worker, officer v. footsoldier. Simón Bolívar, leader of colonial independence in Venezuela, concluded on the basis of the Haitian Revolution "that slave emancipation provided the key to independence." But "even the Liberator assured slaveholders that his policy arose from military necessity and should not be confused with general emancipation. During 1819 and 1820 the patriot army in western New Granada enlisted nearly three thousand Negro slaves, but General Francisco de Paula Santander finally put an end to such recruitment and ordered all negroes not needed by the army to return to the mines" (Davis, *Problem of Slavery*, 81).

28. The phrase is from Mignolo, *Darker Side of the Renaissance*.

29. Davis, *Problem of Slavery*, 304. "The really serious question, which had nothing to do with racial characteristics, was whether emancipated slaves would greatly augment this intractable population? Would the freed black fail to show up for work?" (*Problem of Slavery*, 304).

miration for the discipline of the sugar plantation."[30] Insisting on reading the abolitionist tracts in context, Davis concludes: "As reformers grappled with the problems of crime, pauperism, and labor discipline, they seemed to be unconsciously haunted by the image of the slave plantation . . . Slaveholders and industrialists shared a growing interest not only in surveillance and control but in modifying the character and habits of their workers."[31] Tracing the thread of English abolitionism, Davis is able to show clearly the complexity of Liberty as a principle of social organization, as it wove itself through the fabric of a newly forming industrial society, resulting in "a highly selective response to the exploitation of labor."[32] The success of the abolitionists, ending British slave trade in 1807, coincided with the birth of the idea of "free" labor, destined to become its own form of labor discipline, as earlier legislation protecting British workers was systematically eliminated.[33]

30. Davis, *Problem of Slavery*, 377.

31. Davis, *Problem of Slavery*, 458.

32. Davis, *Problem of Slavery*, 403. Davis insists that the argument linking abolitionism and the societal need for labor discipline "needs to be developed with considerable care and qualification, in order to avoid the simplistic impression that 'industrialists' promoted abolitionist doctrine as a means of distracting attention from their own forms of exploitation," and yet: "The abolitionist movement cannot be detached from its defining social context—from the accelerating pace of enclosures, which augmented a drifting population of rural paupers; from the problem of disposing of convicts, who could no longer be shipped to America; from the trade in pauper apprentices, who were being sent by the wagon- or bargeload from London to the mill towns; from the growing desire for utility, efficiency, productivity, and order; or from the industrial employment of small children, which to the generation of the 1790s, as J. R. Poynter has observed, seemed almost a 'panacea.'" (*Problem of Slavery*, 455–56).

33. Davis observes as significant the fact that "the humanitarian triumph of 1807 coincided, roughly, with the removal of much of the legislation that had protected the traditional customs of trade and the restrictive practices of English workers. By 1809, according to E. P. Thompson, 'all the protective legislation in the woolen industry—covering apprenticeship, the gig-mill, and the number of looms—was repealed. The road was now open for the factory, the gig-mill, the shearing-frame, the employment of unskilled and juvenile labour'" (*Problem of Slavery*, 452). Similarly, writes Davis with sarcasm, in the year (1834) that slavery itself was abolished "nominally" in the colonies, "the Poor Law Amendment liberated the English workers from public welfare and offered the unemployed a choice between starvation and the humiliating workhouse" (*Problem of Slavery*, 357).

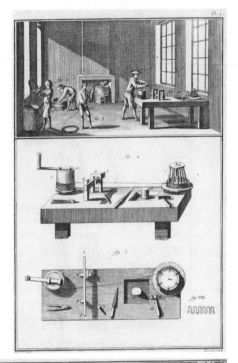

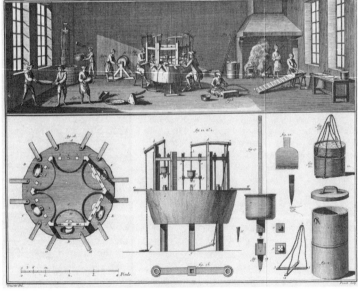

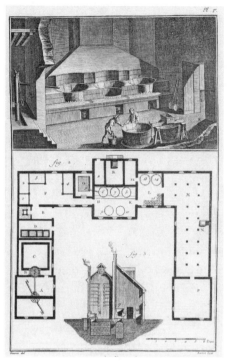

FIGURE 18. Sugar Manufactory (*Sucrerie*), from Diderot and d'Alembert, *Encyclopedie*, vol. 18.

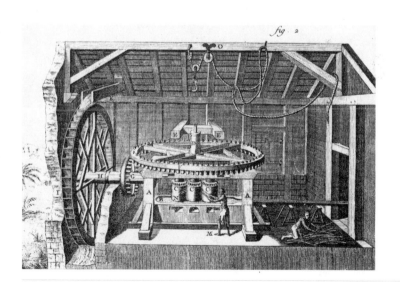

What mattered, then, was not labor exploitation, but sustaining the fiction of voluntary submission to it.[34] The courts "did not condemn industrial slavery as a violation of human rights" in the case of English or Scotch workers "bound for life to coal mines and salt works," because "a worker who accepted token wages could be defined as free, even if in fact he remained perpetually dependent."[35] The ideology of free labor, buttressed in Europe by racist notions of difference, was a defeat for the British working class as, ultimately, freedom became the overarching term for Britain's claims to its own historical superiority as destined to "lead the forces of moral and economic progress."[36] Free property, plus free labor, plus free trade added up to the newly conceived, modern criterion of Liberty. The system of labor emerging in Britain "might have depended on millions of involuntary laborers, but it was, by definition, a 'free world.'"[37]

It is significant that all of this happened *before* the introduction of machine labor on a grand scale. By imagining modernity as synonymous with Europe, we have misunderstood how much modern capitalism was a product of the colonial system, which was in many ways ahead of European developments. Aimé Césaire wrote, "to study Saint-Domingue is to study one of the origins, the sources of Western civilization."[38] But we need to go further with this insight.

34. "If English and Scottish courts had admitted that a man might legitimately consent to become a slave, they would have jeopardized all the legal fictions concerning 'voluntary labor'" (Davis, *Problem of Slavery*, 490).

35. Davis, *Problem of Slavery*, 490.

36. Davis, *Problem of Slavery*, 50. According to Davis, the end of the slave trade was "moral validation" of England's "triumphant commercial empire" (*Problem of Slavery*, 71).

37. Davis, *Problem of Slavery*, 62. "Free trade," the political program of Manchester capitalists in the mid-nineteenth century, meant trade not taxed if it was processed within England for reexport. By late century, this euphemism was abandoned in favor of an explicitly imperialist policy. These ambiguities in the uses of the term "freedom" are not foreign to us today, when the "free world" has become synonymous with deregulation, private property, and "free" labor, and "free trade" has been resurrected as a political platform that often implies an imperialistic agenda.

38. Césaire, *Toussaint Louverture*, 23.

If we allow the Caribbean insurgents their due, Western civilization itself dissolves into a history of the porous and unbounded space in which the insurgents acted.

The Factory Invades Europe

I find it surprising that historians have taken such little notice that the very word "factory," which has become synonymous with industrial progress, was an invention of Europe's colonizing project. Centuries before Manchester's industrial takeoff, the first "factory" was the Portuguese *feitoria*, or trading post, that provided a foothold on the coastal harbors of Africa, a business enterprise totally distinct from the establishments of domestic manufacturing (*fabricação*).[39] The British adopted the term in just this sense. Factories were trading companies in foreign countries or colonies, granted monopolies by royal charter, who sent agents ("factors") to these foreign outposts that functioned as company headquarters, storehouses, and wholesale processing centers. British factories were famous establishments at Hudson's Bay, St. Petersburg, Lisbon, Quidah, and eastward into India.[40] They initiated the modern form

39. It would be fruitful to trace the terms with precision in the languages of the various colonial powers. Adam Smith spoke of the pin-making establishment as a "manufactory"; the French term (from Diderot's *Encyclopedie*) was *epinglier;* the word for a sugar manufactory in the colonies was *sucrerie* (the French word *usine* does not appear until the Industrial Revolution). There seems to be the least differentiation in the American context, where "factory" is used early in the sense of manufactory or *fabrica*— not surprisingly, as the entire country was the product of colonialism—reserving the word "trading post" for its own colonizing project on the Western frontier. Freedom to incorporate domestic industries came slowly in Europe, but was relatively rapid in the United States.

40. The East India Company had a factory in Dacca that manufactured muslin for export, and closed it down in 1818, as the lead in manufacturing cotton textiles moved to England, where machine labor was adopted in the 1820s and 1830s. India suffered huge losses in its sole manufactured export that transformed foreign remittances thereafter into raw materials. India's superior domestic skills in the textile industry were thus effectively destroyed by colonial policy, so that it now imported cotton goods. In the 1850s, English calicoes, replacing those of India, had become the "pillar of British

of corporations, amassing capital through the joint-stock system (prohibited as too speculative for domestic manufacture) that financed the risky business of long-distance "trade," a euphemism for the extraction of value overseas. Factories were agents of imperial projects, sharing real estate with forts and integrally involved in colonial wars. And they were enormously profitable, with no sense of what constituted a "fair" gain, as was the case with domestic production. It is not misleading to understand the first factories of Manchester as an extension of the colonial system, which was now invading the mother country.

"Manchester in 1815 was a warehouse town," undergoing "a pattern of change dominated by wholesale, marketing and exchange, rather than production."[41] The city acquired the name Cottonopolis because of its pivotal position in a global enterprise that connected colonial cotton plantations with spinning yarn destined for reexport, as a wholesale way station to final sale in Europe.[42] This foreign-oriented, merchant business was viewed with distrust by domestic manufacturing firms, who outsourced production to home workers in the surrounding villages, but shared space in Manchester's warehouses that rented to both kinds of enterprises, domestic firms engaged in outsourcing and merchant factories engaged in spinning yarns for foreign trade. It took some time for these two forms

---

Empire" (Farnie, *The English Cotton Industry*, 96–99). For an account of how Hegelian conceptions of World History became "an instrument of the East India Company's colonial project," see Guha, *History at the Limit of World History*, 51.

41. Lloyd-Jones and Lewis, *Manchester and the Age of the Factory*, 32. This monograph of economic history, based on real estate records for the city, reveals the overwhelming importance of the warehouses, rather than the cotton factories they housed, as assets for generating tax revenues. The small scale nature of Manchester's businesses "is lost if we emphasize factory over warehouse; and fail to know that a lot of the spinning firms were small, not large. . . . They were greedy for laborers, but they remained small scale" (*Manchester and the Age of the Factory*, 37).

42. The yarn spun in Manchester was considered "not a manufactured product but a raw material import." It was spun using the labor of women and, even more, children (Lloyd-Jones and Lewis, *Manchester and the Age of the Factory*, 66).

of capitalism to develop a sense and a reality of shared interests.[43] In the revolutionary period that is our focus, this was not yet the case. Nor was highly mechanized production typical of Manchester factory labor.[44] What is being suggested here is that when the modern labor force is considered without the divisions of nation, or race, or even political status of slave versus free, there is a remarkable coherence and continuity to its development.

That coherence was not without contemporary observers, but it has taken until our own era of globalization for historians to think to tell history from their perspective. In a tour de force of Atlantic scholarship, Peter Linebaugh and Marcus Rediker have pieced together the lived experience and political perceptions that were shared by the "motley crew" of workers in the seventeenth and eighteenth centuries, the "multiple figures" of the propertyless, laboring classes that formed the "Atlantic proletariat": seamen, slaves, indentured servants, foot soldiers, the "hewers of wood and haulers of water" who built the ports, sailed the ships, clear-cut the forests,

43. "Certainly, the rapid diffusion of the power-loom from the mid-1820s did reconcile the differences . . . but this could not be seen in 1800, any more than it was a foregone conclusion in 1815. The rate of diffusion of the power-loom in the first two decades of the nineteenth century was snail pace . . . There is little doubt that there was a separation of interests between spinners and manufacturers c. 1800–1820; a clash of interests that could take on an extreme form." It was not until the 1820s that class interest triumphed, and "Manchester's business community" achieved "internal coherence, rather than being at loggerheads with each other." This process was aided by horizontal integration of the two types of firms and significant use of power looms in manufacturing as well as spinning, a form of integration that involved a convergence of the warehouse building and the factory enterprise. Before then, "it is a simplification to assume the identification of a factory to a single building" (Lloyd-Jones and Lewis, *Manchester and the Age of the Factory*, 16, 64).

44. Lloyd-Jones and Lewis note that emphasis on power machinery as the determining element denies the basic structural feature of industrial (as opposed to colonial) capitalism, the fact "that the worker is free and not a slave. Factory workers of the Industrial Revolution owned their labour power" (*Manchester and the Age of the Factory*, 84). Similarly, Davis, following Stephen A. Marglin, notes, "it was not technology that led irresistibly to the creation of a concentrated and dependent force of wage laborers. In many industries, at least, it was the entrepreneur's new social and managerial role that required continuous supervision of employees and control over the proportions of their work and leisure time" (*Problem of Slavery*, 459).

fought the wars, and worked the fields, and who posed a constant threat of escape or insurrection to claim their freedom—precisely the underclass of both involuntary laborers and masterless men that so troubled the forces of law and order in colony and mother country alike.[45] If the new regime in Haiti did not acknowledge the connections and commonalities between modern slavery and modern free labor, the motley crew did.

The Motley Crew

Linebaugh and Rediker's study, *The Many-Headed Hydra*, focuses on the British-dominated Atlantic, making visible the role of the laboring classes in building the new global order by documenting instances of their rebellion against it. Prototypical of the multiethnic, motley crew were sailors, thousands of whom, domestic and foreign, were impressed or otherwise dragooned into service on the ships of the British merchant fleet. "Factory ships" moored off the African and Asian coasts were "a forcing house of internationalism," providing "not only the means of communication between continents, but also the first place where working people from these different continents communicated."[46] Ship mutinies were political acts. Pirate crews became multiracial, multiethnic "hydrarchies," self-governing counterregimes that administered justice, shared wealth, and waged war.[47] In cities along the colonial coasts, runaway slaves joined with European immigrants as self-organzing cells of waterfront rebels, who formed the radical wing of the New York City

45. Linebaugh and Rediker, *Many-Headed Hydra*.
46. Linebaugh and Rediker, *Many-Headed Hydra*, 151–52. Atypically, these authors pay attention to the fact that the "very term *factory* evolved etymologically from *factor*, 'a trading representative,' and specifically one associated with West Africa, where factories were originally located" (*Many-Headed Hydra*, 150).
47. Linebaugh and Rediker, *Many-Headed Hydra*, 142–73.

insurrection of 1741 as well as the American War for Independence (the authors describe George Washington and the property-owning and slave-holding elites as counterrevolutionaries in comparison).[48]

Linebaugh and Rediker link seventeenth-century witch hunts, the exile of religious dissenters, enclosures of the commons, and harsh punishment for property crimes as acts of repression by power hierarchies that spanned both sides of the Atlantic.[49] They trace the metaphor of the many-headed hydra, the Biblical monster that grew two heads for every one successfully severed, that cropped up repeatedly in this period to describe protest movements by communist levelers, religious antinomians, insurrectionary slaves, and revolutionary radicals. "The motley crew thus provided an image of revolution from below that proved terrifying. . . . Elite colonists reached readily for images of monstrosity, calling the mob a 'Hydra,' a 'many-headed monster,' a 'reptile,' and a 'many-headed power.' Many-headedness implied democracy run wild."[50] The rebels' actions were not, however, without organizational and theoretical coherence. Citing the writings of their spokespeople who, they claim, gave voice to the motley crew as a whole, Linebaugh and Rediker insist on the enlightened consciousness of these traveling historical actors: "This multi-ethnic proletariat was 'cosmopolitan' in the

48. Linebaugh and Rediker, *Many-Headed Hydra*, 178, 206, 211–47.

49. Following Silvia Federici, they describe the criminalization of "independent female prophesy" as reaching a peak between 1550 and 1650, "simultaneously with the Enclosures, the beginning of the slave trade and the enactment of laws against vagabonds, in countries where a reorganization of work along capitalist lines was underway" (Federici, cited in Linebaugh and Rediker, *Many-Headed Hydra*, 52). See also Federici, *Caliban and the Witch*.

50. Linebaugh and Rediker, *Many-Headed Hydra*, 233–34. On antinomianism: "This hydra had too many heads to be crushed at once" (*Many-Headed Hydra*, 282). Note that General Leclerc, head of the invading French force in Saint-Domingue, registered the same concern when he wrote home to Napoleon: "It is not enough to have taken away Toussaint, there are 2,000 leaders to be taken away" (James, *Black Jacobins*, 346). Toussaint is reported to have said upon his capture, "In overthrowing me, you have cut down in San Domingo only the trunk of the tree of liberty. It will spring up again by the roots for they are numerous and deep" (*Black Jacobins*, 334).

original meaning of the word."[51] Not racist nationalism, but global humanism was their message.

Whereas David Brion Davis describes how the legal arguments of abolitionists "drove a wedge" between liberty and labor, slave workers and free, these authors discover radical thinkers who made the inexorable link between colonial slavery and slavelike labor conditions of domestic English workers, and spoke out for the abolition of them both.[52] The Irishman and "proletarian theorist," Edward Despard, who met his African-American wife Catherine when he was a soldier in the American colonies, was convicted and hanged as a traitor in the 1790s for plotting a London conspiracy to promote, in the judge's words, "the wild and Levelling principle of Universal Equality."[53] The mulatto Methodist minister Robert Wedderburn, who warned British colonial planters that "the fate of St. Domingo awaits you," and interpreted the Biblical Jubilee as a promise of political and economic liberation in colony and metropole alike: after the Peterloo Massacre of Manchester demonstrators in 1819, he advocated arming the English proletariat.[54]

In the Age of Revolution, such proponents of "universalism from below" spoke of one race, the human race, an idea articulated far more broadly than the later course of history would have it appear. Olaudah Equianno, Lydia Priest Hardy, Thomas Hardy, William Blake, Thomas Paine, and Constantin François Volney were writers who described themselves as "citizens of the world."[55] Their radically cosmopolitan writings circulated throughout the globe as counter-texts to the official version of history wherein "universalist claims of

51. Linebaugh and Rediker, *Many-Headed Hydra*, 246.
52. Davis, *Problem of Slavery*, 376; Linebaugh and Rediker, *Many-Headed Hydra*, 305.
53. Linebaugh and Rediker, *Many-Headed Hydra*, 281, 248–86.
54. Linebaugh and Rediker, *Many-Headed Hydra*, 313–14, 320, 287–326.
55. Volney traced civilization to African origins, and celebrated "the motley appearance" of human diversity, "a most extraordinary and most attractive spectacle," raising "the motley crowd to a universal ideal" (Linebaugh and Rediker, *Many-Headed Hydra*, 343).

revolution shrank to a narrow, racialist nationalism."[56] Linebaugh and Rediker, contemporary cosmopolitans and champions of the newest victims of global exploitation, express regret at the failure of this "conspiracy for the human race": "What was left behind was national and partial: the *English* working class, the *black* Haitian, the *Irish* diaspora."[57]

2. History Out of Bounds

The Politics of History Writing

Linebaugh and Rediker's history would seem to complement the work of Davis, who traces many of the same issues from the perspective of British legal theory and abolitionist writings, as it demonstrates that in some cases at least, the connection *was* made between slavery and free labor, transcending racial difference. It comes as a surprise, then, that these authors clashed sharply in the public sphere when Davis's essay that was critical of *The Many-Headed Hydra* appeared, evoking a harsh retort from Linebaugh and Rediker. While Davis appreciated the "Atlantic perspective" of their book, writing that some parts "deserve high praise," including "fascinating personal stories" (of the Despards, Wedderburn, and others), he condemns the authors' scholarship as full of factual errors and misleading interpretations, which he attributes to their "Marxist" message. In reply, Linebaugh and Rediker charge Davis with "red-baiting."[58]

Both descriptions miss the mark. *The Many-Headed Hydra* is in fact a major challenge to Marxist orthodoxy in its whole conception of the proletariat as preindustrial and Atlantic in scope, its emphasis

56. Linebaugh and Rediker, *Many-Headed Hydra*, 134.
57. Linebaugh and Rediker, *Many-Headed Hydra*, 286.
58. See Davis, "Slavery—White, Black, Muslim, and Christian"; Rediker, Linebaugh, and reply by Davis, "An exchange." The following citations are from the Internet postings; hence, no page references are given.

on the importance of women leaders, sympathy for Christian radicals, concern with race as much as class, and aversion to vangardism as a form of political organization.[59] The book's subject, moreover, is a *failed* revolutionary movement of proletarian workers against merchant-capitalist exploitation, not any iron laws of class struggle or industrial-capitalist development.[60] For his part, Davis, who counts himself among those "well to the left of center," is not condemning the writers for their political concerns but, rather, for the political effects of their presentation. He is wary of writing that politicizes history as a morality story of good and evil that misses the contingencies and complexities of events, the imperfect knowledge and unintended effects of human actors, and turns history into a romanticized struggle between heroes and villains. His wariness is not without reason, given the political abuses to which historical accounts by the Left *and* the Right have sometimes led. But in this reprise of a Cold War scenario wherein one side retreats to the standards of the profession and the other resorts to charges of red-baiting, their heated exchange leaves the reader strangely untouched. This old, New Left standoff seems irrelevant to the experience of actually reading the works on both sides of the debate.

59. In fact, Linebaugh and Rediker are remarkably free of class reductionism, as their account focuses not on actions reflecting capitalist class interests or proletarian class violence but, rather, on the motley crew's "persistent efforts, against great violence, to organize practical alternatives to capitalist forms of social organization" (Rediker, Linebaugh, and reply by Davis, "An exchange"). Davis's own narrative of the ideological obfuscations of "free labor" is in certain ways conceptually closer to the Marxist historical tradition.

60. In their words: "The book seeks to recover two hidden histories. First the endless mutilations and executions, the terror, and the killing labors used by the ruling classes of the day against European, African, and American workers in building Atlantic capitalism. The violence was greater than most historians have been willing to acknowledge. Second, and more hopefully, the connections among the multi-ethnic workers of the Atlantic as they as they resisted the violence. The linkages were more important than most historians have been able to see—because of the blinding effects of concepts of race, class, and nation that have guided most accounts of the past" (Rediker, Linebaugh, and reply by Davis, "An exchange").

No one can defend sloppy scholarship. Although human error will never be eliminated completely (and although the first efforts in a field will be most vulnerable, lacking the corrective powers of later commentary), a quasi-neurotic compulsion for accuracy is an occupational necessity for history writers, the minimum responsibility that she or he has when asking for a reader's trust. But Linebaugh and Rediker are right to insist that something else is at stake besides professional standards. In making too strong a distinction between fact and ideology, truth and distortion, Davis is skirting the more basic issue as to the meaning of historical inquiry. It takes us, unavoidably, deep into the philosophy of history, and its central question: how are we to make sense out of the temporal unfolding of collective, human life? The need to rethink this question today in a global context, that is, as *universal* history, has not been felt so strongly for centuries—perhaps not since Hegel, Haiti, and the Age of Revolution.

Why do we write history? What truth is it evoked to reveal? Here the facts, which may or may not be carelessly reported, are incapable in themselves of providing an adequate answer. Moreover, because the central question of history's meaning cannot be asked outside of time but only in the thick of human action, the way the question is posed, the methods of the inquiry, and the criteria of what counts as a legitimate answer all have political implications. Davis has, indeed, a philosophy of history, the source of which can be traced to the European Enlightenment that understands knowledge production as critique. Facts, for Davis (in his many, excellent books on Western slavery) *are* a politics, the goal of which is demythification. His rigorous scholarship rubs against the grain of the popular misconceptions that are woven into official history and used by those in power to justify their present dominance. Linebaugh and Rediker want to go a step further, however, not only unsettling the dominant account but producing another, a counternarrative that does more than criticize the status quo; it inspires action to change it. Their explicit aim is to connect today's global resistance to an earlier one, "retrieving the proletarian body from its monster articulation" (the hydra),[61] and linking Louverture, the Despards, Wedderburn, and others to the "planetary wanderers" of today, "ever ready from Africa to the Caribbean to Seattle to resist slavery and restore the commons."[62] Countermyth is myth all the same, Davis would argue, and he is right to point out the dangers. But a strict, positivist empiricism is not an option in historical cognition, because facts without concepts are meaningless. England is a concept, not a fact, as are "Europe," "Enlightenment," "economy," "progress," and "civilization." Whether or not such concepts are mythical is a collective, evaluative judgment that changes historically. This *is* the political issue precisely.

Who or what is the collective subject of history? Is it the nation? Civilization? Class? Is it Hegel's cunning actor, Reason? Each of these categories of comprehension, while determining present phenomena as meaningful, comes to us full of residues of the past, containing the sedimented history of utopian dreams and cultural blind spots, political struggles and power effects. Historically inherited concepts form the collective consciousness of actors who, in turn, create history. Paradoxically, even when collective actors proclaim themselves as the standard-bearers for universal history—indeed, especially when they make this avant-gardist claim—they establish their identity in contrast to others, to outsiders. This brings our inquiry back to the thought with which the essay, "Hegel and Haiti," came to a close. Is it possible to reimagine universal history out of bounds of exclusionary conceptual frames? Can we humans, in a kind of reversal of Hegel, refuse to see ourselves as

61. Rediker, Linebaugh, and reply by Davis, "An Exchange."
62. Linebaugh and Rediker, *Many-Headed Hydra*, 353.

history's instrument, our particular actions meaningful only when subsumed within some overarching concept as it historically unfolds —even when that concept is human freedom? Can collective subjectivity be imagined as inclusive as humanity itself? Is there a way to universal history today?

Porosity

The first step would be to recognize not only the contingency of historical events, but also the indeterminacy of the historical categories by which we grasp them. This step was taken by historians like Paul Gilroy, whose attempt to grasp the diaspora of Africans across the black Atlantic led him to argue that no identifying concept of race or nation is adequate. The collective experiences of concrete, particular human beings fall out of identifying categories of "nation," "race," and "civilization" that capture only a partial aspect of their existence, as they travel across cultural binaries, moving in and out of conceptual frames and in the process, creating new ones. Porosity characterizes the ordering boundaries of their world (as it does ours today). Ethnic identities mislead political judgments when they are based on the "unthinking assumption that cultures always flow into patterns congruent with the borders of essentially homogeneous nation states."[63]

63. Gilroy, *Black Atlantic*, 5. Against a nationalistic "overintegrated" conception of cultures as "immutable, ethnic differences," and modernity as an "absolute break in the histories and experiences and experiences of 'black' and 'white' people," this book proposes "another, more difficult option: the theorization of creolisation, métissage, mestizaje, and hybridity. From the viewpoint of ethnic absolutism, this would be a litany of pollution and impurity. These terms are rather unsatisfactory ways of naming the processes of cultural mutation and restless (dis)continuity that exceeded racial discourse and avoid capture by his agents" (*Black Atlantic*, 2). Dayan (among others) has criticized Gilroy's affirmation of hybridity, making slavery, racism, and economic exploitation a metaphor, and thereby losing sight of the inhumanity and brutality of the colonial slave system, and the continuation of violence against Blacks today (Dayan, "Paul Gilroy's Slaves, Ships, and Routes," 8). My argument here is a different one.

A dialectic is in play. Turning our attention to the porosity of concepts in turn gives semantic power to the concept of porosity, marking certain facts as significant. It suddenly matters that Dutch merchants carried Spanish trade and settled in Portuguese colonies.[64] "Fifteenth-century Portugal . . . is a metaphor."[65] Perhaps more than half the "British" navy was not British.[66] Among indigenous Americans: "Two-thirds of the Oneida were Algonkin and Huron in 1669. The Jesuits even complained that it became difficult to preach to the Iroquois in their own language."[67] Napoleon's "French" army sent to restore slavery in Haiti included Germans and Poles. Trade societies connected cities rather than land masses; territorial borders were routinely ignored, and smuggling was ordinary business.[68]

Porosity, unlike hybridity, does not name a cultural form. It insists, rather, that the lived experiences of the New World for the colonial dominators *and* the slaves (as well as indigenous populations), in every case challenged preexisting conceptual distinctions. Granted, their experiences were radically unequal in pain and suffering, reflecting the brutally racist inhumanity of the capitalist, colonial project; nonetheless, in every case, they necessitated those who lived through it to reimagine their world.

64. Compare with Simon Schama's stress on national cohesion (see above, "Hegel and Haiti," section 2): "The Netherlands is so much a land of immigrants that the very definition of 'Dutch' is problematical" (Blakeley, *Blacks in the Dutch World*, 3).

65. Portugal described "what actually was a mixture of political and economic forces, both national and supranational in origins. The term 'Portugal,' while symbolizing a nation, has as well obscured these forces and their significance" (Robinson, *Black Marxism*, 145). "We begin to perceive that the nation is not a unit of analysis for the social history of Europe" (*Black Marxism*, 25).

66. The navigation laws of the seventeenth and eighteenth centuries attempted to control this tendency.

67. Wolf, *Europe and the People Without History*, 167. "Many of the Indian 'nations' or 'tribes' later recognized as distinct ethnic entities by governmental agents or by anthropologists took shape in response to the spread of the fur trade itself, a process in which the native Americans were as much active participants as the traders, missionaries, or soldiers of the encroaching Europeans" (*Europe and the People Without History*, 194).

68. "Tea was being blithely smuggled across the 'unbreachable frontiers' of England until 1785" (Braudel, *Civilization and Capitalism*, 3:294). Braudel stresses the porosity of urban centers: "Lisbon, and through Lisbon the whole of Portugal, was under the partial control of foreigners" (*Civilization and Capitalism*, 3:141); in Antwerp, "foreigners dominated the scene—Hanseatic traders, English, French and above all southern merchants: Portuguese, Spanish and Italian" (*Civilization and Capitalism*, 3:145). Braudel describes early-

The concept of porosity, exposing ungovernable connections, is relevant to feminist issues. The word "commerce" in multiple languages has a sexual meaning. Traffic in women was the prototype of commercial slavery.[69] Sexual commerce was precisely what threatened to dissolve the conceptual boundaries of race, leading to the invention of elaborate subcategorizations of degrees of "racial mixture," and the concept of "unassimilatable" groups that proclaimed the social death of certain kinship alliances classified as miscegenation.[70] It was as threats to conceptual distinctions that fears of contagion arose.[71] Napoleon ordered Leclerc to expel from Saint-Domingue all white women who had slept with blacks.[72] Such fears were not merely psychic fantasies, but rooted in the actual, boundary-disrupting potential of women's sexual agency that was

---

modern Europe's economy in its relation to state power in language that could be applied to contemporary globalization: "[A] gulf developed between nation-states on the one hand, the locus of *power*, and urban centres on the other, the locus of *wealth*" (*Civilization and Capitalism*, 3:288).

69. The slave-trade in women, sold into prostitution, is a booming business of contemporary globalization. See http://www.protectionproject.org.

70. I am drawing here from the study by Patterson, *Slavery and Social Death*, who notes that in cases when slavery is "intrusive," that is, when as aliens they are brought into society and are not assimilated (via adoption), they experience social death. One of Patterson's references is the work of the French anthropologist Meillassoux, who discusses slavery as the "antithesis of kinship," and distinguishes the social impact of slaves on kinship alliances from economic exploitation of slave labor: "Slavery, *as a mode of exploitation*, exists only where there is *a distinct class of individuals*, with the same social state and *renewed constantly and institutionally*, so that, since this class fills its functions permanently, the relations of exploitation and the exploiting class which benefits from them can also be regularly and continually reconstituted" (Meillassoux, *Anthropology of Slavery*, 36). Biological reproduction across the categories of alien, slave, and free cannot mean a kinship alliance; in a society where women are exchanged to form marriage alliances, and where social status is inherited from the father, the system of reproducing an economically exploited slave class is put into jeopardy by the free mulatto daughter of a white planter and black slave woman; on the other hand, the pairing of a white planter-class woman with a black slave results in the loss to whites of the social value of her reproductive power.

71. Literal contagion was the source of this metaphor's power, as "the sugar colonies [became] a melting pot for diseases from Europe, Africa, and the New World" (Braudel, *Civilization and Capitalism*, 3:40).

72. Sala-Molins, *Le Code Noir*, 275.

economically powerful and escaped political control. The figure of the free, mulatto woman looms large here, brilliantly interrogated by Joan Dayan in her history of Haiti.[73]

The lived experience of the Atlantic as an expanded social field, shared by millions of heterogeneous, previously unconnected people, threatened every existing order of collective meaning. No cultural heritage could be transported across the Atlantic without undergoing a radical transformation. Porosity characterized the existential boundaries of what was for all participants indeed a New World. Its reorganization would be the consequence of violence. But in the indeterminacy of transition, new perspectives began to take shape. Multiple efforts were made to produce knowledge adequate to the time, attempts that dug deeply into various historical traditions in order to reinvent them. As histories were reimagined along human networks that were sexual, social, economic, and political all at once, mythic impulses necessarily played a role. Constellations of people whose mutual recognition was unprecedented attempted to think this new world as meaningful, leading to a spurt of cosmological speculation. When philosophy of history emerges in this way, universal humanity is its thematic.

Limited Horizons

Writing in 1798 toward the end of his life, Kant described with uncharacteristic passion how the French Revolution had inspired public sentiment with the idea that people had the right to self-rule by a constitution of their own making. Observers took the side of the revolutionaries even when it went against their private interests or pecuniary gain. This "drama of great political changes," despite "misery and atrocities . . . has aroused in the hearts and desires of

73. Dayan, *Haiti, History and the Gods.*

all spectators who are not caught up in it a sympathy which borders almost on enthusiasm." The historical experience of such collective enthusiasm "can never be forgotten," even if the revolution were to fail, because it bears witness to "a moral disposition within the human race" that is a source of hope for the historical progress of humankind: "[A] view opens up into the unbounded future."[74]

That such enthusiasm characterized the young Hegel's reception of the Saint-Domingue Revolution, is the claim of "Hegel and Haiti." As spectator via the press (newspaper names like *Spectator* and *Observer* were common[75]), Hegel achieved glimpses of a global perspective, viewing the uprising of the slaves of Saint-Domingue as a manifestation of *universal* freedom, the realization of which he saw as the very structure and meaning of history. Once Hegel had grasped this meaning, however, he demonstrated little patience with the mere matter of empirical history, dismissing it as "lazy existence" (*faule Existenz*).[76] Concept took precedence over content, and attention to historical facts was overwhelmed by Hegel's enthusiasm for the philosophical system itself.

Hegel, an armchair observer who never left the shores of the continent, was poorly positioned to see beyond Europe's horizon when he developed a "Philosophical History of the World."[77] His idea of dialectical synthesis, the supercession of conflicts and contradictions within an overarching rational development embodied in the secular state, was a departure from church narratives of apocalyptic time, but it held onto the Christian teleology of a divine plan.

74. Kant, "The Contest of Faculties," 182–85.
75. Such names were common in colonial newspapers (for example, the Saint-Domingue *l'Observateur colonial*) as well as in Europe.
76. For a critique of Hegel's dismissal of "lazy existence," see Adorno, *Negative Dialectics*, 8.
77. "The subject of this course of Lectures is the philosophical History of the World" (Hegel, *Philosophy of History*, 1). Hegel traveled extensively in Germany and Switzerland in his youth, but did not visit Paris, Belgium, the Netherlands, Austria, and Italy until the 1820s. He frequently waxed romantic about sea travel, but he was an observer from the shore.

His philosophy explicitly affirmed Protestantism in the guise of Reason, and his dismissal of human happiness as history's thematic retained elements of Christian worldly asceticism.[78] He saw the practice of politics (in which the actions of great men substitute for miraculous intervention) as the instrument of this progress, and imagined the stage for its realization on a global scale. Europe and European-colonized America were, he believed, history's dominant agent in "the modern time," justifying the colonizing project as the development of Reason in the world.[79] The West was declared the historical avant-garde for all humanity progressing necessarily toward a common end.[80]

Robert Bernasconi has analyzed the multiple variants of Hegel's lectures on the *Philosophy of History* during the 1820s and compared them with the sources on Africa that he consulted, demonstrating how Hegel allowed his schema of history to take over from fact by ignoring counterevidence that did not fit his formula for progress.[81] Hegel described sub-Saharan Africa, which he called "Africa proper" (*das eigentliche Afrika*), as "isolated," which as his sources knew from the Muslim trade routes was not the case, and "unhistorical," that is, static and unchanging in time.[82] Bernasconi argues against many

78. "The History of the World is not the theatre of happiness. Periods of happiness are blank pages in it, for they are periods of harmony—periods when the antithesis is in abeyance" (Hegel, *Philosophy of History*, 26–27).

79. Hegel, *Philosophy of History*, 83–87, 412–57.

80. "The material existence of England is based on commerce and industry, and the English have undertaken the weighty responsibility of being the missionaries of civilization to the world; for their commercial spirit urges them to traverse every sea and land, to form connections with barbarous peoples, to create wants and stimulate industry, and first and foremost to establish among them the conditions necessary to commerce, vis. the relinquishment of a life of lawless violence, respect for property, and civility to strangers" (Hegel, *Philosophy of History*, 455).

81. Bernasconi, "Hegel at the Court," 41–63. A critical-historical edition of these lectures does not exist (for details, see above, "Hegel and Haiti," 73n139).

82. Bernasconi, "Hegel at the Court," 43. "'Africa proper' [*das eigentliche Afrika*] is introduced before the account of world history gets underway . . . in order that it can subsequently be left behind" ("Hegel at the Court," 60). Africa "served as a nullpoint" ("Hegel at the Court," 52).

scholars that the cultural racism permeating Hegel's philosophy cannot be excused by blaming his scholarly sources.[83] Rather, when paraphrasing the experts (Karl Ritter, T. E. Bowdich and others), Hegel was "not reliable" as a copyist.[84] He "embellished" the stories of cannibalism and human sacrifice and was "compelled to multiply the numbers," indulging in distortions and exaggerations to serve his philosophical purpose of making a certain developmental scheme seem logical.[85] Despite his very partial knowledge, Hegel approached Africa "with systematic intent" in order to construct a philosophy of history based on ascendance from the "sensuousness" (*Sinnlichkeit*) of fetish-worshipping Africans to the superiority of Christian spirituality.[86] His schema provided "a potent justification" for the later exploitation of the African continent by Europeans.[87]

83. "An examination of Hegel's sources shows that they were more accurate than he was and that he cannot be so readily excused for using them as he did" (Bernasconi, "Hegel at the Court," 63). Bernasconi's judicious analysis is a needed corrective to my own blunt rhetoric in "Hegel and Haiti," that "Hegel was in fact becoming dumber" by reflecting "Europe's conventional scholarly wisdom on African society" (see above, "Hegel and Haiti," 73–74).

84. Bernasconi, "Hegel at the Court," 45. We know this tendency of Hegel already from his careless citing of the numbers in Adam Smith's example of the pin factory (see above, "Introduction to Part One," 5n3).

85. Bernasconi, "Hegel at the Court," 51–52, 63.

86. Bernasconi, "Hegel at the Court," 51–58. Hegel argued that Africans lacked "a sense of something higher than man," and "did not regard slavery as improper"— hence "the beneficial effects of Africans' exposure to European culture, even if this began in the position of slaves." Slavery was wrong, but "by taking Africans out of Africa as slaves, Europeans had already released them from a barely human existence, even if they were not yet free" ("Hegel at the Court," 58). "So even when Blacks revolt against slavery, as they did successfully in Haiti, this would seem, in Hegel's view, to be because they have come in contact with European views about freedom" ("Hegel at the Court," 61).

87. Bernasconi, "Hegel at the Court," 59. "Barbarism is a fault to be corrected, if necessary by violent means. . . . Hegel believed generally that so-called 'civilized' peoples could legitimately interfere with those at a lesser stage of development. . . . Colonialism was the destiny to which Africa had to submit" ("Hegel at the Court," 59). "[B]y giving a positive role to the enslavement of Africans by Europeans from the perspective of human development, he gave comfort and resources to those who rejected abolition. It is no wonder that the owners of slaves in the United States saw him as an ally" ("Hegel at the Court," 58).

The Ashanti chief Kwak Dua told a British governor in 1842: "I remember when I was a little boy, I heard that the English came to the coast of Africa with their ships for cargoes of slaves for the purpose of taking them to their own country and eating them; but I have long since known that the report was false."[88] Given Hegel's intentionally exaggerated accounts to his gullible European audience of the bloodthirsty Ashanti, Kwak Dua appears truly reasonable in contrast. But the point of returning to the historical moment in which Hegel incorporated Haiti into a European story that excluded Africa as insignificant is less to condemn the German philosopher than to take a step in redeeming ourselves.[89]

While few today would define themselves as Hegelian, his assumptions are still widely shared. Violent political action determines what matters in the collective history of humanity. The idea of progress justifies the imposition of democracy on others as a military project. The division of humanity into advanced, civilized peoples and those who are backward and barbaric has not been abandoned.[90] The purportedly secular schema of universal history as one path, forged by the developed (Christian) nations, which the whole world is destined to follow, is still ingrained in Western political discourse. Cultural racism has not been overcome.

There is no scientific reason to evaluate human collectives according to some social-Darwinian criterion of mere survival.

88. Told to Winecott, cited in Bernasconi, "Hegel at the Court," 49. Kwak Dua acknowledged the practice of human sacrifice, arguing that the power over life and death was the prerequisite for sovereign rule: "If I were to abolish human sacrifices, I should deprive myself of one of the most effectual means of keeping the people in subjection" ("Hegel at the Court," 49). His argument is positively Schmittian (see Schmitt, *Political Theology*). The Ashanti fought bitter wars against the British until their final defeat in 1896.

89. Bernasconi writes, "the reader of Hegel . . . must ask him- or herself about the extent that he or she remains captive to this account" ("Hegel at the Court," 44).

90. Bernasconi's conclusion shares these concerns: "Questions remain about the extent to which contemporary ideas as, for example of social development, remain tied to a model that can best be described as colonialist" ("Hegel in the Court," 63).

Rather than collective wisdom being the product of civilizational dominance, these two variables may as well be inversely correlated: The greater the power a civilization wields in the world, the less capable its thinkers may be to recognize the naiveté of their own beliefs. Humanity can do better.

3. A New Humanism

Atlantic Cosmologies

Kant's mind filled with "admiration and reverence" when gazing at the stars.[91] Hegel, with more hubris, was indifferent. The poet Heinrich Heine recalled visiting with the now famous philosopher in Berlin, when they stood at the window and Heine expressed enthusiasm for the starry night. "The stars, harrumph," grumbled Hegel, "the stars are only a gleaming leprosy on the sky."[92] For those who endured the Atlantic crossing, however, the stars were survival itself. Before the invention of the marine chronometer to measure longitude, Atlantic sailors were at the mercy of the starry heavens, guided by the southern constellation known as the Hydra, the ancient sign of mariners.[93] The origin of slaves sold in the Americas was ascertained through their recollections of the positions of the stars during their land journeys to the African coast.[94]

91. He compared the awesome sublimity of stargazing to feeling "the moral law within," experiences marking the limits of the sensual world from the most infinite to the most personal (Kant, *Critique of Practical Reason*, 203).

92. Cited in Blumenberg, *Genesis of the Copernican World*, 71.

93. Linebaugh and Rediker, *Many-Headed Hydra*, 353. The marine chronometer, invented by the clockmaker and amateur scientist John Harrison (who received official recognition in 1773), was installed widely in ships only in the late eighteenth century. See Sobel, *Longitude*.

94. Attempts were made to find where the slaves were from by asking "how many days they were underway, how many markets they were sold at *en route*, on what side of their march the sun rose and set, or to ask whether their country was to the left or the right of 'this star'" (Debien, *Les Esclaves aux Antilles français*, 37).

Astrological signs figured centrally in New World spatial reckoning. But the time of the heavens was a clumsy tool for speculations on human history, whereas evidence from multiple cultures was visibly at hand. There was no common language in the New World, no phonetic system of shared meanings. This was true among the African slaves as it was among the motley crew—or the American colonialists, for that matter.[95] Freemasonry thrived in this environment. The Masonic movement initiated a fascination with nonverbal means of communication, a search for universal human knowledge in signs, symbols, artifacts, and past architectural wonders, interpreting them esoterically as the secret source of wisdom.[96] A visual world of images, from Egyptian pyramids to indigenous Indian sign language, was queried for possible keys to a common humanity that existed before the Biblical fall of Babel.[97]

In the porous space of the transatlantic, the links of Masonic belonging were often stronger than those of country, ethnicity, and even race, and they are vital for an understanding of historical events

95. Haitian creole, like other creoles, developed as a "contact language," as did the "pidgin" languages spoken by motley crews. Its evolution is not well documented, given ignorance of linguistics generally until the twentieth century. It is now (with French) the official language of Haiti. Based primarily on French (just how close to the colonial planter class French it was is a matter of debate), it contains elements from Fon (as ethnolinguistic substratum), Ewe/Anlo-Ewe, Wolof, and Gbe (all from the Niger region), as well as Bantu (from Kongo), and Arabic (via Islam). See Anglade, *Inventaire Etymologique*.

96. Masonry, inspired by European experiences of global travel, believed in the illuminating potential of other traditions, particularly those of the Middle and Far East (Jewish mysticism, Zoroastrianism, Egyptian paganism, Sufi mysticism, Hindu Vedanta). Masons were equally at home with occult knowledge (secret rituals, medieval alchemy, and Renaissance magic) and the secular Enlightenment (experimental science, free press, democratic governance), as well as active participants in the public sphere, contributing to a transnational network of publications. They are a side of the Enlightenment that Habermas's influential account leaves out (Habermas, *Structural Transformation of the Public Sphere*).

97. For Masonic speculation on Indian sign language, see Denslow, *Freemasonry and the American Indian*. The birth of speculative Freemasonry in the eighteenth century owed at least as much impetus to New World cultural mixing as it did to the initiation of archaeological excavations into Europe's ancient origins. Indeed, these endeavors ran parallel, as Europeans believed they were viewing their own primitive past in present-day, preliterate ("prehistoric") peoples.

in the Age of Revolutions. But generalizations prove difficult. What precisely does it mean to say that Freemasonry flourished in the New World?[98] Lists of the lodges and historical actors who were members tell us little in themselves. The numbers, while impressive, are substantively ambiguous and circumstantially misleading, fueling the myth of a global conspiracy of Freemasonry still alive today. There are multiple Masonic realities, varying in time, and their social roles have differed greatly. To *be* a Mason is an ontological category empty of defining qualities for which it could be held causally responsible (just as to be a Christian does not make one virtuous, to be a Marxist does not make one a revolutionary, to be a Muslim does not make one a terrorist). Freemasonry is the paranoid's empty signifier. While there were internal uniformities and shared secret knowledge within the movement, modern Masonry, founded in the eighteenth century, contained inherent contradictions. Toussaint became a Mason, but so, allegedly, did Napoleon who destroyed him.[99] The brotherhood was a society of equals, but it was organized in a hierarchy of merit, and social equality generally stopped at the lodges' door. Masons traced a metaphoric genealogy back to stone builders and handworkers; in practice, they were neither. They were, rather, "social architects," but this too could mean many different things. All were champions of cosmopolitanism,

98. Lodges dotted the Caribbean as well as the American colonies. They were "a familiar feature in colonial Saint-Domingue" among white colonialists (Nicholls, *From Dessalines to Duvalier,* 23); and were reestablished in black Haiti as a fundamental association of civil society. In the Age of Revolution, they existed as well in Haiti, Martinique, Nicaragua, Antigua, the Virgin Islands, Bermuda, Honduras, Granada, Dominica, the Bahamas, St. Thomas, Trinidad, Cuba, Mexico, and the Creek and Cherokee Indian nations of the north-continental southeast (thanks to Richenel Asano and Linda Rupert for this information).

99. Napoleon is alleged to have become a Mason in Malta in 1798; while that claim is in some dispute, it is clear that he was sympathetic to the movement and appointed its members to high places. His 1798 military adventure in Egypt strengthened this association, as his occupying officers introduced the lodges there. Freemasonry has since been an attachment for many French heads of state. It remains for many a symbol of European imperialism, attracting as members colonial (and postcolonial) elites.

enthusiastically embracing the idea of global brotherhood.[100] Some were radically inclusive in their membership.[101] But only a minority were racially mixed, others exclusively black.[102]

All lodges practiced civic virtues as a training ground for citizenship. The members' withdrawal from society allowed dissent from the dominant cultural ethos, and encouraged utopian thinking for which the world outside was not ready—structural elements that understandably made civil authorities nervous. Lodge secrecy was inherently political, as membership provided transnational loyalties, alternative social identities and competing sources of authority. But political affinities spanned the spectrum: British lodges in the early eighteenth century were consciously opposed to political activism, Austrian lodges for a time boasted royalty as sponsors, while others, like those discussed in "Hegel and Haiti," spawned armed revolutionaries.[103]

100. American Indians, initiated into London lodges as Masons, joined the British side against American Revolutionaries; Masons on all sides are alleged to have shown leniency to fellow Masons captured as prisoners during this struggle and the French and Indian War.

101. In Carpentier's well-researched historical novel set in the Caribbean (in which the historical figure and Mason, Ogé, makes an appearance), the politically radical Foreigners' Lodge had "a healthy democratic atmosphere" where European nobility "could mix familiarly with a coloured patriot from Martinique, a former Jesuit from Paraguay, homesick for his mission-station, a Flemish typographer, expelled from his country for printing propaganda or an exiled Spaniard, a peddler by day and an orator by night, who claimed that freemasonry had already been active in Avila in the sixteenth century, as was proved by certain designs of compasses, set squares and mallets, recently discovered—according to him—in the Church of Our Lady of the Assumption, built by the famous Jewish architect Mosén Rubí de Braquemonte" (Carpentier, *Explosion in a Cathedral*, 102–3).

102. Some of these had long and important histories; for example, Prince Hall Mason's Lodge begun in Puerto Rico, that in New York in the late-nineteenth century included Shomburg, a black Puerto Rican, who negotiated the "transcultural difference" of multiple identities as black, Mason, Afro-Hispanic, Caribbean, and "Guarionex," his revolutionary pen name that was the name of an Indian chief from Santo Domingo convicted by the Spanish colonial authorities for his uprisings who died in 1502 (see Arroyo, "Technologies," 4–25).

103. See above, "Hegel and Haiti," 62–65. The lodge that Mozart joined in Vienna in 1784 was for socializing and drinking, as opposed to those that created revolutionary networks. Hapsburg Emperor Joseph II was initially sympathetic to the movement as

Freemasonry spread with colonization, but colonization changed it. Perhaps the most important aspect of this context was the need to trust strangers in a strange land. "Lodges first started in the seaports and trading communities as commercial clubs or business references."[104] Masonry, like other secret societies, created fictive kinship relations, providing mutual aid for brothers of the lodge (Cuban black lodges raised money to free slaves).[105] They were exemplary of secret societies throughout history that have spread along trade routes, where business transactions cross community lines, and traditional social affinities are insufficient for building reliable human networks.

"Has freemasonry contributed its share to the ceremony of vodou? So it is said," writes the anthropologist Alfred Métraux in his study of the Haitian religious cult.[106] Vodou has changed over time, and in its relation to Haitian Freemasonry. But contemporaries

---

a builder of national patriotism, but by 1785 he feared it was becoming too powerful. The connections between Mozart's opera *The Magic Flute* and Freemasonry are now well known. The famous architect Karl Friedrich Schinkel designed the scenery for the production of *The Magic Flute* that opened in Berlin in 1816, one year before Hegel began his professorship there. Mozart's last completed work, K623, is known as "Little Masonic Cantata," dated 15 November 1791. The words appear to have been written by Mozart himself, for the inauguration of a new temple: "Es umschlänge diese Kette; es wie diese heilige Stätte/Auch den ganzen Erdenball." See Landon, *Mozart and the Masons*.

104. Lipson, *Freemasonry in Federalist Connecticut*, 7.

105. Benjamin Franklin, himself a Mason, wrote: "They speak a universal language and act as a passport to the attention and support of the initiated in all parts of the world . . . they have made men of the most hostile feelings, and most distant religions, and the most diversified conditions [Jews, Muslims, blacks, American Indians] rush to the aid of each other, and feel social joy and satisfaction that they have been able to afford relief to a brother Mason" (cited in Clawson, *Constructing Brotherhood*, 77).

106. Métraux, *Le Vaudou haïtien*, 140. Métraux, born in Switzerland and educated in Paris, was a contemporary of the generation of Parisian Surrealists who held a fascination for Vodou, among whom some, like Michel Leris, viewed practitioners not as the primitive "other," but as a phenomenon of modernity that destabilized the very notion of otherness, the idea of distinctly separate cultures upon which conventional ethnographies were based. Insisting on the theatricality of its rituals, Métraux believed Vodou should be studied not as an exotic and primitive remnant, but as a place of overlap, clash, and creation, an urban religion of "the other West." See J. Michael Dash, "Le Je de l'autre," *L'Esprit Créatur*, 47, 1 (2007): 84–95. My position is in sympathy with Métraux.

FIGURE 19. Vodou ceremony
(1970). Photo by Leon
Chalom. From Dayan, *Haiti,
History and the Gods.*

of the Age of Revolution perceived Vodou as "a sort of religious
and dancing masonry" with reason, given its embrace of strangers
and syncretic epistemology.[107]

The millions of slaves brought to the New World, often por-
trayed as an undifferentiated mass, were as varied in language, re-
ligion, customs, and political institutions as European populations
in the colonies. While it is true that the massive influx of slaves to
Saint-Domingue in the decades just prior to the revolution were
shipped predominantly from the coasts of the Kongo and Benin,
they were brought there from multiple locations in the interior as
prisoners of wars waged against and among each other—the great
Kongo civil wars that had raged for a century and reached a peak in

107. See above, "Hegel and Haiti," 65n129.

FIGURE 20. Masonic initiation ceremony,
late nineteenth century.

the 1780s, and the multiple wars waged by Dahomey (now Benin)
against the Oyo and other neighbors with alternating outcomes and
increasing intensity.[108] These onetime enemies, enslaved on the
battlefield and sold via indigenous merchants to Europeans as human
merchandise, underwent a kind of extraordinary rendition, force-

108. "It is worthy of consideration, after all, that perhaps as many as two-thirds
of the slaves in Saint-Domingue (Haiti) on the eve of the revolution had been born,
raised, and socialized in Africa," including some 62,000 Kongolese exported during
the decade of 1780–1790 (Thornton, "'I am the Subject of the King of Congo,'" 183).
The Kongolese had been torn by civil war since the mid-seventeenth century. The Oyo
Empire was won at the expense of the Benin peoples to the east, so that by the late-
eighteenth century, it controlled over half of what was later named Yorubaland. For an
account of the significance of this generation's experience of battle and the form of
military tactics that made the slave insurgents so successful, see Thornton, "African
Soldiers in the Haitian Revolution," 58–80.

ful transfer out of their native jurisdictions that amounted to torture by proxy. It was the shared trauma of defeat, slavery, banishment, and the horrors of the Atlantic crossing and plantation labor that Vodou, in a burst of cultural creation, transformed into a community of trust.[109]

Vodou was public religion as well as a secret society. Like Freemasonry, given the need to communicate visually when common language was lacking, emblems, secret signs, mimetic performance, and ritual were fundamental. And like Freemasonry, shared knowledge was envisioned as an amalgam of elements drawn from a whole variety of human cultures, open and additive, rather than hierarchically closed. Cosmological speculation proceeds differently here than with abstract reasoning. The philosophical principle is syncretism rather than synthesis, correspondences across nonidentical cultural fields. The worldly residue, the matter of what Hegel called "lazy existence," is never overcome. In contrast to Hegelian synthesis where contradictory terms fall under an overarching concept, signs remain distinct, disjointed, molecular, connected rhizomically within the whole. The boundaries of these meaning systems are porous. There is no edge to Masonic or Vodou emblematics, and in this sense they could, and did, bleed into each other. The orthodox cross, the builders' compass, the rainbow and the serpent, the skull and crossbones, were emblems shared by Vodou and Freemasonry. And yet these New World practices were far from identical, not because of some essential "otherness" of African humanity, but because of the essentially *inhuman* experience of modern slavery. Métraux insists: "The political and social frameworks peculiar to the African tribes from whom the Haitians of today are descended, *were pulverized by slavery*."[110] There is nothing comparable in European Freemasonry.

109. There are related phenomena; Candomblé (in Brazil), Santaría (in Cuba, Puerto Rico, and Panama), and Shangó (in Trinidad).
110. Métraux, *Voodoo in Haiti*, 59 (my emphasis).

The Allegorical Mode

Emblems are silent signs, meaningful only when interpreted, and here the mode of interpretation is decisive. Vodou was constructed out of the allegorical mode of seeing that experiences history as catastrophe.[111] For those who have been defeated by history, whose social relations have been severed, who live in exile, meaning drains out of the objects of a world that has been impoverished by physical distance and personal loss. In Vodou, the collective life of not one but multiple cultures has been shattered, surviving as debris and in decay. Emblems are hollowed out; their meanings have become arbitrary.[112] The skull and crossbones—a variant of the pervasive emblem of the deaths-head—signifies not merely the transiency of life, but the transiency of meaning, the impermanence of truth itself.[113] The gods are radically distant. They have deserted the living. They must be recalled, physically reembodied, literally "possessing" the body of a believer at every Vodou ceremony, just as the elaborately

111. This understanding is indebted to Walter Benjamin, for whom "[a]llegory was the mode of perception peculiar to a time of social disruption and protracted war, when human suffering and material ruin were the stuff and substance of historical experience" (Buck-Morss, *Dialectics of Seeing*, 178).

112. The objects in the world, emptied of traditional meaning, can be filled by the residues of multiple contents. Rather than pointing to a transcendent truth, they are signs of the fungibility of meaning—an image of snakes being driven by St. Patrick from Ireland is transformed into "multiple embodiments of the [sacred Dahomean] serpent of the sky" (Thompson, *Flash of the Spirit*, 176)—or, they might be discarded altogether. This process of the decay of meanings may have started already in Africa as a consequence of the social disruptions of wars, to a considerable degree driven by the slave trade. Hegel refers to observers' comments that Africans threw away their "fetishes" that disappointed as evidence of the arbitrariness (hence, in his view, primitiveness) of their systems of belief. One would need to question his presumption that such had always been the case. Was this practice, rather, the consequence of the disintegration of African cultures whose economic and political base was affected by the European slave trade?

113. The appearance of the same sign in very different contexts here points not to symbolic unity, but to the allegorical arbitrariness of meanings. In the eighteenth century, the skull and crossbones was an emblem of the Prussian military *and* pirate ships, an insignia of the British troops that also appeared on George Washington's Masonic apron. In the nineteenth century, this sign lost its emblematic power when its meaning was fixed by international convention as the sign of poison.

conceived *vèvès*, the Vodou cosmograms figured on the ground in poured powder and erased by the dancers' feet, must be created every time anew.[114]

This is the allegorical experience; in it, culture exists as ruins. In contrast, Freemasonry's cosmological speculations are situated in the transhistorical realm of symbols, the goal of which is uncovering eternal truths. Knowledge is sought not from cultural fragments of the recent past, but from the grand monuments of ancient eras and remote civilizations. When it comes to emblematics, symbols aim toward timelessness and systemic wholeness: "Freemasonry taught that . . . men should seek to build a Temple of Humanity in which all valuable knowledge would be enshrined, and where the lost past would be remembered."[115] Such confidence in the permanence of meanings is the luxury of those at home in the living present, for whom the forward march of time appears as progress, and history remains intact despite material decay—an experience antithetical to that of African-American slaves.

There have been impressive ethnographic studies identifying the reappearance of African religious and social elements within Haitian cultural forms.[116] I do not mean to imply that in the New World nothing remained of original intent. But it is inconceivable, from a human point of view, that these brutally enslaved and expa-

---

114. See above, figure 11. It is striking that these images produced on the ground of Vodou temples are an intentionally transitory form of sacred art. They have no future. "Everywhere in vodon[sic.] art, one universe abuts another," writes Thompson, who describes the content of the *véves* as "geometric thought." He attributes to the geometric form of the *véves* a unity of contents as well: "In other words, this is more than a crisscross of the earth at point of contact with the sky. In effect, this *véve* complex provides geometric focus for a constellation of Dahomean, Kongo, and Roman Catholic forces constituting the very fabric of Haitian cultural history" (Thompson, *Flash of the Spirit*, 191, 116.) The point made here is that Thompson's interpretation of textual wholeness is utopian rather than real, and to a great extent the fictional creation of later commentators.

115. Curl, *Art and Architecture of Freemasonry*, 136.

116. Leaders in this field are Melvile J. Herskovits, John M. Janzen, Robert Farris Thompson, and John K. Thornton.

triated persons carried their rituals and gods with them in slave-ship holds like so much checked baggage, as if arriving on a diplomatic mission of cultural exchange. Dahomean (Fon) and Yoruban (Nâgo) deities indeed reappear alongside Kongo divinities in the Haitian pantheon, both interchangeably with Roman Catholic saints, but their loss of unique aura, their fungible equivalence, implies a profound transmutation of their powers.[117] Herskovits has traced the Haitian *zombi*, phantasm of the living dead, to Dahomean legend.[118] But Dayan is surely right to argue that this figure, "a soulless husk deprived of freedom" and "the ultimate sign of loss and dispossession," takes on unprecedented meaning in response to colonial slavery's "peculiar brand of sensuous domination," and the conditions of forced, free labor that followed Haitian independence.[119]

What does it mean to call the North Kongo secret societies of *Lemba* the "rightful source"[120] of the Haitian Vodou practices of the same name, when the former was an organization of slave traders, and Vodou practices were performed by the very individuals they sold? The Bantu word *Lemba* means "reconciliation," "maintaining peace" in both cases, but in wildly different contexts. African *Lemba* healed personal and social afflictions that were the consequence of

117. See Thompson, *Flash of the Spirit*, 166–67, for a list of the equivalent Yoruba, Fon (of Dahomey), and Haitian names of the gods. The *loa* (deities) of Kongo origin include Simbi, Nkita, and Mbumba.

118. Herskovits, *Dahomey*, 243.

119. Dayan, *Haiti, History and the Gods*, 37. As "the most powerful emblem of apathy, anonymity, and loss," the *zombi* "tells the story of colonization"—as well as "the twentieth-century history of forced labor and denigration that became particularly acute during the American occupation of Haiti" (*Haiti, History and the Gods*, 37). "The lwa [*loa*] most often invoked by today's vodou practitioners do not go back to Africa" (*Haiti, History and the Gods*, 36).

120. "[Robert Farris] Thompson [see *Flash of the Spirit*] is the first to identify *Lemba's* rightful source in connection with Haitian religion as the north-Kongo healing cult by the same name" (Janzen, *Lemba*, 280). Janzen acknowledges that the historical link is "tenuous"; still, the structural similarities cannot be denied (*Lemba*, 278). See Janzen, *Lemba*, 53, for a discussion of the seventeenth-century Kongo *n'kisi* in the coastal slaving port of Loango that protected the dead against witches who would drag off their souls to slavery and forced labor.

FIGURE 21. Hector Hyppolite, "An Avan, An Avan!"
(Forward, Forward!), c. 1947.

material gains from the Atlantic trade in guns and slaves (eleven
guns, "obsolete castoffs from European arsenals," were the equivalent
of one human enslaved as the consequence of wars spurred on by the
arms trade[121]). Operating along inland trade routes, *Lemba* emerged
among mercantile clans that formed a network stretching from
the coastal cities deep into the slave-producing interior.[122] Its elite
members, "wealthy (or wealth-acquiring) and influential merchants,

121. Janzen, *Lemba*, 34.
122. Janzen, *Lemba*, 34. Closely connected with the trading clans of the *Vili* of
north Kongo, the *Lemba* cult practiced in the coastal port of Logano among "a sedentary
commercial elite in touch with European traders" connected to "the endpoint of the
trade" by mobile traders carrying portable *Lemba* shrines inland (*Lemba*, 54, 324).

judges, healers, diviners, and chiefs,"[123] were endowed with priestly functions such as sanctifying marriage alliances, upholding market laws, ritualistically redistributing wealth, and performing the ideological magic of conflict resolution and social control.[124] Its members were "persons driven, even obsessed with success in trade, influence, and public prestige."[125] In a society possessing "a strong egalitarian ethic," their trading practices led to the multiple social maladies that *Lemba* was called upon to heal.[126]

African *Lemba* was ritual expiation. It assuaged the guilty conscience of wealthy traders and mitigated the jealousies of the unsuccessful, preventing the region's social fabric from being totally destroyed by the Euro-Atlantic trade. If, as Janzen and others argue, striking continuities can be discerned between *Lemba* practices in Old World and New, then there were radical *dis*continuities in their historical roles. African *Lemba* produced the miseries that New World slaves endured. The task of reconciliation among the slaves shipped to Saint-Domingue, hardly an issue of redistributing wealth, concerned building fraternal alliances of trust among former enemies

123. Janzen, *Lemba*, 317.

124. *Lemba* was a nonstate movement to shape the public order along transport routes rather than political centers. Initiation marriages were key to bringing unity and alliance among traders: "There is no doubt . . . that the *Lemba* therapeutic ideology was a model for a fully-formed social state"; as "the major transcending institution of the region from the seventeenth century to the twentieth century, [it] apparently played the key role of creating a ceremonial context for the economy of trade to mesh with the economy of agricultural production, and a context in which to generate medicinal symbolism to assuage the lives of those at the intersection of the two economies" (Janzen, *Lemba*, 321, 323).

125. Janzen, *Lemba*, 317.

126. Janzen, *Lemba*, 318. "The clan alliances consecrated by *Lemba* constituted a network of socio-political relationships across a vast region, in particular the inland routes of the international trade . . . [of slaves and guns that] required some form of social control. Such wealth and influence as this brought introduced strong currents of envy and jealousy . . . touching off in the minds of these wealthy and influential persons such symptoms as dreams, nightmares, fears of sorcery, attack, sterility, death, and a host of other specific symptoms." These are the *Lemba* afflictions among "individuals coming to terms with the coastal trade" (*Lemba*, 317–18).

of war and among persons massed together in labor gangs who had no common background and little understanding of each other, indeed, they may not have known of each other's cultural existence before the crossing.

If *vèvès* and altar arrangements in Haitian Vodou temples replicate in miniature the cosmograms paced out by *Lemba* members on African meadows, if the names of the Dahomean divinities reappears in the dominant Rada cult of Vodou *loa*, in short, if the words and the structure of cultural *language* remained, what was said in this language in response to historical events was totally new.[127] This is nowhere more obvious than in the case of the secret societies of warriors that are said to have played a part in the Haitian Revolution.[128] Warrior societies existed in Kongo, in Dahomey, and elsewhere in Africa, but their purpose was never to initiate an event of slave insurrection. On the contrary: "The slave trade intensified the Dahomean warrior way of life," because prisoners of war were sold to the traders.[129] None of Vodou's precedents in Africa ever conceived of eliminating the institutional arrangement of master and

127. Janzen summarizes the scholarship on African influences in Haiti: "Both in ritual observance and in scholarship the dominant West-African influence is acknowledged to be that of Dahomey, as witnessed by the cultic vocabulary of spirits (*loa*), cult complexes (*voudou* [sic.]), cult leadership (*houngan, mambo*), cult locations (*hounsi*), and so on, although even here there is the possibility of Kongo influence. . . . Dahomean deities are collectively known as Rada (from the slaving port town Arada, itself named after Allada), whereas those of Kongo and Bantu origins have recently been identified as strongly reappearing in the Pétro cycle of deities" (*Lemba*, 277). But Dayan cuts to the core of what matters when she writes: "Petwo gods that bear the names of revolt, the traces of revenge, like Brisé Pimba, Baron Ravage, Ti-Jean Dantor, Ezili-je-wouj (Ezili with red eyes), and Jean Zombi, recall the strange promiscuity between masters and slaves; white, black, and mulatto; old world and new. These rituals of memory could be seen as deposits of history. Shreds of bodies come back" (*Haiti, History, and the Gods*, 35).

128. This is not to deny Thompson's claim that the success of the warriors can in large part be explained by their former warrior experience. "Looking at the rebel slaves of Haiti as African veterans rather than as Haitian plantation workers may well prove to be the key that unlocks the mystery of the success of the largest slave revolt in history" (Thornton, "African Soldiers in the Haitian Revolution," 74).

129. Thompson, *Flash of the Spirit*, 165. Thompson marvels at the continuities between cultures in the Old and New World. "The Yoruba remain the Yoruba" despite the

slave altogether. No European nation did either. The radical anti-slavery articulated in Saint-Domingue was politically unprecedented.

The definition of universal history that begins to emerge here is this: rather than giving multiple, distinct cultures equal due, whereby people are recognized as part of humanity indirectly through the mediation of collective cultural identities, human universality emerges in the historical event at the point of rupture. It is in the discontinuities of history that people whose culture has been strained to the breaking point give expression to a humanity that goes beyond cultural limits. And it is in our empathic identification with this raw, free, and vulnerable state, that we have a chance of understanding what they say. Common humanity exists in spite of culture and its differences. A person's nonidentity with the collective allows for subterranean solidarities that have a chance of appealing to universal, moral sentiment, the source today of enthusiasm and hope. It is not through culture, but through the threat of culture's betrayal that consciousness of a common humanity comes to be.

At the Crossroads

The rightful source of Haitian religious practice is the experience of slavery, leading to the insurrection of 1791. The rightful source of universal history, however, is not in the specifically Haitian articulation of that event—even less in its absorption by narratives of the French Revolution. Universality is in the moment of the slaves' self-awareness that the situation was not humanly tolerable, that it marked the betrayal of civilization and the limits of cultural understanding, the nonrational, and nonrationalizable course of human

---

diaspora, reflecting "the triumph of an inexorable communal will" (*Flash of the Spirit*, 16). Given the fact that "Yoruba culture" is itself a cultural invention of the late nineteenth century, this presumption of permanence lacks credibility (see Matory, "The English Professors of Brazil," 72–103).

history that outstrips in its inhumanity anything that a cultural outlaw could devise.[130] At the same time, we are pushed to the point where Hegel's dialectic of master and slave falls silent. Self-awareness must lead to action, *and yet* action endangers precisely what is at stake in the idea of universal humanity. The dilemma of the insurgent, then as now, is that violent resistance, apparently justified by moral sentiment, sets the stage for new brutalities that are repugnant to that sentiment, because against the enemy of humanity, every barbarism is allowed. What dialectical understanding, what political struggle will provide liberation from *this* contradiction?

Historical judgement, when called upon to take sides, reenacts this moral dilemma. The slave ceremony at Bois Caïman that initiated the insurrection provides the practicum (see figure 22). Written sources of this event of August 1791 in the north of Saint-Domingue are scant and unreliably remote. Just what happened, or even *if* it happened, is endlessly disputed.[131] Yet as the originating moment of the Haitian Revolution, it is cited as historical proof of all conflicting claims. These fragments: a conspiracy; a mass meeting at night at Bois Caiman; slaves assembled in the forest; a fiery speech by a huge black man called Boukman; a blood oath of brotherhood; a sacred ceremony led by a black priestess called Fatiman; the slaughter of a black pig; ritual singing and dance. Days later, the violence begins. Was this meeting an "authentic" Vodou ceremony?[132] Was it a "blending" of African traditions, and if so, with what motive?[133] Was the dance simply the pretext used by the leaders to distribute arms and issue passwords to the work gangs, aware that rumors of

130. Is it presumptuous to attribute to the slaves an awareness of the universality of the event as an answer to Dayan's critical lament: "Where, oh where do we find the slave's point of view?" ("Paul Gilroy's Slaves, Ships, and Routes," 8).

131. See Geggus, "Bois Caïman Ceremony," 41–57.

132. "With only slight exaggeration, one can say that the reputation of vodou as a unifying and revolutionary force begins with the ceremony of Bois Caïman" (Geggus, "Bois Caïman Ceremony," 51). Geggus considers this reputation itself exaggerated.

133. Geggus, "Bois Caïman Ceremony," 51.

FIGURE 22. Ulrick Jean-Pierre, *Painting entitled Bois Caïman 1 (Revolution of Saint-Domingue, Haiti, August 14, 1791),* 1979. Oil on canvas, 40 × 60 in. Collection of Dr. and Mrs. Jean-Phillipe Austin, Miami, Florida.

Vodou would terrify the planters?[134] Was it an act of "revolution from below," the "self-sustained activity of the masses?"[135] Was it a case of premodern laborers breaking out of traditional forms of peasant resistance, finally aiming to overthrow the system of slavery itself?[136] Or, was the ceremony initiated by elite leaders whose use of certain African motifs was "calculated to mobilize support"?[137] Did this event indicate elaborate organization, or the lack of it? Was it "a revolt that broke out prematurely," an unauthorized break in discipline before the conspiracy was supposed to start?[138]

And what of the ideology of the insurrection? Was it news from Paris, perhaps the Declaration of the Rights of Man that emboldened the insurgents? Or was the French Revolution peripheral even for the leaders, as it was "liberty for all," not French republicanism they desired?[139] The view that the Bois Caïman blood pact was specifically Dahomean is "difficult to reconcile" with the fact that Kongo slaves were in the majority in the area, where a KiKongo political chant was recorded on the eve of the revolution.[140] The "Good Lord" evoked in Boukman's exhortation has been identified as pagan, specifically, the lead god of Dahomey, but the Kongo majority had been officially

---

134. Fouchard, *Haitian Maroons*, 224.

135. This is the subtitle of the book by Fick, *Making of Haiti*. "It was . . . the self-sustained activities of diverse segments of the population, of largely unknown and obscure individuals, as well as the popular leaders . . . that made the defection [from France] of Dessalines, Christophe, Clervoux, and the other colored generals both practicable and militarily meaningful" (*Making of Haiti*, 248–49).

136. Genovese, *Rebellion to Revolution*; compare to Fick, *Making of Haiti*, 61.

137. Geggus, "Bois Caïman Ceremony," 51. Not only field slaves, but house slaves and free blacks were united in the insurrection, an indication that social status was not determining; rather, it was the desire for liberty.

138. Geggus, "Bois Caïman Ceremony,"47.

139. Fouchard, *Haitian Maroons*, 224. Compare to Dubois, *Avengers of the New World*, 107. Dubois considers Bois Caiman as "shorthand for the complex and varied presence of religion in the planning and execution of the insurrection" (*Avengers of the New World*, 101).

140. Geggus, "Bois Caïman Ceremony," 50. The chant, also the subject of minute debate, is alleged to address the Kongo deity Mbomba (rainbow). It contains

Christian since Portuguese Catholic missionaries converted the Kongo king in 1491.[141]

All of these interpretations have been put forward of an event that may not even have happened. It is almost as if it *had* to happen for interpretation to exist at all. Bois Caïman has assumed signifying power for political judgments that are radically diverse. It is used to mean that Haiti entered into modernity proper because it joined the European story, the only story that counts. Or, it means that with Haiti, history has surpassed this narrative, leaving Europe behind. Or, it means that Haiti has become a nation—like other nations, like Europe, complete with its own military honors, pedigree of "founding fathers," and bloody birth through the sovereign sacrifice of human life. This fight for ownership of Haiti's past revolutionary glory diverts attention from Haiti's deplorable present reality. It seems crude to discuss Haiti as a bastion of historical significance, when today it is the poorest nation in the Western Hemisphere, and when expressions of the political will of the Haitian people continue to this day, *after two hundred years*, to be hamstrung by the intervention of foreign powers.

In its early experience of impoverished dependence on the global economy, in its early struggle against Western policies of genocide, and in its postcolonial, hierarchical articulation of social elites, Haiti indeed stands at the vanguard of the history of moder-

---

the key word "*kanga*" that in all KiKongo dialects means to "tie" or "bind," (although among Christians from Kongo it might also mean "to save, protect, or deliver"), and it has political significance in Kongo. It has been translated: "Eh! Eh! Mbomba [Rainbow] hen! Hen! / Hold back the black men / Hold back the white men / Hold back that witch / Hold them. [*Kanga li.*]." For a thorough discussion of the ambiguities of translation, hence the difficulties of interpretation, see Thornton, "'I Am the Subject of the King of Congo,'" 210–13).

141. Although the official Catholic Church supported the planters, certain Jesuit priests acted to defend individuals who engaged in violent acts against their masters (for example, attempts at poisoning). See Fick, *Making of Haiti*, 65.

nity.[142] The Haitian experience was not a modern phenomenon *too*, but *first*. Haiti's founding fathers used a discourse of nationalist unity ideologically to push the freed slaves back into conditions of plantation labor and production for export, a specifically modern political strategy that is hardly outdated. Haitian elites were the first in history to embrace the word "black" as their political identity, a position totally compatible then (and now) with social hierarchies based on the color of one's skin.[143] If radically cosmopolitan Freemasons once championed the cause of slave liberation, Haitian national Freemasonry, like the movement worldwide, has long been at peace with the status quo of power. Haitian political leaders persecuted Vodou priests even before independence. (Under Toussaint's orders, Dessalines slaughtered over fifty Vodou practitioners, whose own definition of the insurrection threatened their monopoly of power.[144]) Vodou practice was pushed to the margins, an embarrassment for "modern" Haitian elites, yet it has remained a way of manipulating the poor peasantry, hence a source of power for political oppositions of every persuasion. To narrate Haiti's history as good versus evil stunts our capacity for moral judgment. Past suffering does not guarantee future virtue. Only a distorted history is morally pure.

Inhumanity in Common

Where in this discourse is the critical intellectual to find a foothold? Is it enough to have rescued the Haitian story from absorption into Eurocentricity? Can we rest satisfied with the call for acknowledging "multiple modernities," with a politics of "diversality," or "multi-

142. The French seriously considered the suggestion that in order for the memory of the insurrection to be obliterated, all existing slaves would need to be exterminated, and fresh slaves brought to replace them. See Fick, *Making of Haiti*, 220–23.

143. See Nicholls, *From Dessalines to Duvalier*, chap. 1, for a discussion of the persistence of this "colour prejudice."

144. Trouillot, *Silencing the Past*, 37–40, 66–69.

versality," when in fact the inhumanities of these multiplicities are often strikingly the same? Critical theoretical practice today is caught within the prisonhouse of its own academic debates. We are confined within the globally extended theory world, as artists are within the globally incorporated art world. It is no use deflecting *our* struggle for hegemony onto the past, playing it out on the backs of historical actors long ago silenced by death. They cannot talk back when we proclaim them heroes or villains in our particular narrative of the past.

Today cynicism easily seduces the younger generation of academics. If their search for historical truth leads to "dizzying" ambiguity, if time is nothing but "indeterminacy and flux," then why not simply succumb to the historical amnesia that the political culture industry is constantly peddling?[145] Why not just make up the past according to one's own convenience, particularly when a recent president of the United States of America has provided such a stunning example of the power-gaining and power-retaining effectiveness of this technique?

Critical thought is empowered by the facts only by being pushed over the brink of the discursive worlds that contain those facts. Let us return to the nighttime meeting at Bois Caïman. The huge black man called Boukman speaks these words: "Throw away the image of the god of the whites who thirsts for our tears, and listen to the voice of liberty, which speaks in the hearts of us all (*couté la liberté li palé nan coeur nous tous*)."[146] The source for this address is dubiously secondhand, but its authenticity has wide support among historians.[147] It complies with the liberty narrative of black Jacobinism; it shows admirable autonomy from the pro-royalist Catholic priests. And if

145. Palmié, *Wizards and Scientists*, 140. Palmié, a virtuoso of theoretical discourse, is exemplary as an advocate of what can be described as an *ontology* of indeterminacy, one that in fact reduces historical interpretation to the most simplistic thesis imaginable (all meaning is indeterminate; all reality is complex). History is flattened out, eliminating the possibility of a dialectical encounter with the past.

146. Geggus, "Bois Caïman Ceremony," 49.

147. This is reported by a slave witness. Geggus believes it may have been at the meeting of leaders before Bois Caïman ("Bois Caïman Ceremony," 52).

FIGURE 23. Jacques-Louis David, "The Tennis Court Oath at Versailles," n.d. Sketch.

Bois Caïman can never be contained within bourgeois space, if Boukman's call for solidarity has an intensity that overpowers the revolutionary oath taken in an indoor Paris tennis court, then it is still legible within the narrative of universal liberation, as that story has been traditionally told.

But what if you learn that Boukman, born in English-speaking Jamaica, was named Boukman—Bookman—because he was literate and could read *the* Book, but that the Book was not the Bible? What if the facts indicate that Boukman, the huge black man who spoke these celebratory words at Bois Caïman, "listen to the voice of liberty which speaks in the hearts of us all," who inspired armed insurrection against the slave masters, was born and raised a Muslim—as were between 4 and 14 percent of all Africans who made the Atlantic crossing;[148] as was the priestess Fatiman—Fatima—who presided over the so-named Vodou ceremony at Bois Caïman; as was the slave Makandal, their maroon rebel predecessor, whose hand had been amputated as a consequence of slavery, and who was accused in the colonial courts of plotting to poison the families of planters in Saint-Domingue in the 1750s and burned at the stake (the Christian punishment for heresy)?[149]

148. Specifically, on Saint-Domingue: "Between the sixteenth and the nineteenth centuries, approximately 6.85 percent of the Africans imported into Saint Domingue were from Senegambia; another 4.5 percent hailed from Sierra Leone; and slightly under 4 percent were from Mozambique. These zones represent the areas from which Muslims were most likely to come to Saint Domingue, in declining order of likelihood . . . and certainly there were Muslims exported from the Bight of Benin (accounting for 27 percent of the total), although in the latter case the captive-producing holy war of Usuman dan Fodio in what would become northern Nigeria would only begin in 1804, so that it would be several years before the number of Muslims coming from the Bight of Benin would be significant. It is therefore reasonable to assume that Muslims in Saint Domingue could have been no more than 10 percent of the enslaved population, and was probably far less" (Gomez, *Black Crescent,* 83). "The Maroon leader Macandal can best be described as a *marabout* warrior" (Diouf, *Servants of Allah,* 152). Boukman, killed in battle, was decapitated, his head "garishly exposed" on a stake in the public square (Fick, "Saint Domingue Slave Insurrection," 25). Such acts of colonial lesson teaching, intended to deter rebellion, had the opposite effect.

149. "He [Makandal] was supposedly brought up in the Moslem religion and apparently had an excellent command of Arabic. . . . According to one version, Makandal

The fact that Muslims, a small but frequently educated minor-
ity of plantation slaves, often preferred for that reason as domestics,
were leaders of New World slave rebellions (most clearly in Bahia in
1835) has been known but not attended to.[150] Highlighting their
presence plants a small intellectual bomb causing the politics of
Western interpretation to bifurcate almost immediately. One path
leads into the temptation to slough off the less palatable aspects of
the slave rebels' behavior, attributing these to the influence of Islam,
for example, the avenging justice of the racial slaughter of whites re-
gardless of civilian status.[151] In this budding, counterterrorist narra-
tive, the observed fearlessness with which the Saint-Domingue slave
rebels rushed into death on the battlefield with what planters de-
scribed as "suicidal fervor," becomes a variant of suicide bombing.[152]

There is a second option. We can accept Boukman as a preacher
of jihad. But if we take this path, then the time-honored critical
narrative of radical liberty is exposed to a precarious extension.
When defenders of Haiti, their moral sentiment ablaze with en-
thusiasm, cite Dessalines's justification of racial slaughter, "I have
avenged America," when intellectuals exonerate the slaves, defend-

---

turned fugitive after his hand was amputated, having caught it in the machinery of the
sugar mill while working the night shift" (Fick, *Making of Haiti*, 60). "Moreau de Saint-
Méry observed . . . that among the Congolese catholicized by the Portuguese were some
who also retained ideas of 'Mohametanism' and 'idolatry'" (Fick, *Making of Haiti*, 291).
See also James, *Black Jacobins*, 20–22, and also Fouchard, *Haitian Maroons*, 141, 184.

150. On the presence of Muslims among the slaves in the New World, see Gomez,
Black Crescent and Diouf, *Servants of Allah*. On Muslim slaves in Saint-Domingue, see also
the following: Fouchard, *Haitian Maroons*, 141, 184; Dayan, *Haiti, History and the Gods*, 245;
Debien, *De l'Afrique à Saint Domingue*, 7. On Bahia, see Réis, *Slave Rebellion in Brazil* (the Bahia
rebels wanted to free themselves, not *all* slaves).

151. Even sympathetic accounts acknowledge the terrible tortures and cruelty in-
flicted on the white populations. Citing C. L. R. James and Eugene Genovese in sup-
port, Fick writes, "as atrocious as they were, these acts of vengeance were surprisingly
moderate . . . compared with those of cold-blooded, grotesque savagery and sadistically
calculated torture committed by their oppressors throughout the past" (Fick, "Saint
Domingue Slave Insurrection," 21).

152. See Geggus, *Haitian Revolutionary Studies*, 78, who is, however, skeptical of the de-
scription of the fervor as "suicidal."

ing Dessalines for setting out "to give as good as he got," then there is no honest reason for excluding from the story of Liberty the eye-for-an-eye, tooth-for-a-tooth logic of political jihad—only the dishonest one of rejecting, not the *means* of jihad, not the policy of violent retribution against one's enemy, but the religious goal, as if to say that in the broadly inclusive panoply, the multiversality of global cultures, there is *one* (with which over a billion human beings happen to identify) that is simply, irredeemably, wrong.[153] The political question emerging from this historical encounter, that urgently needs to be addressed, is this: how is it that the revered Euro-American revolutionary slogan, "Liberty or Death," came to be cordoned off in Western thought and practice from the allegedly infamous tradition of Islamic jihad?

In the name of universal humanity, the vanguard justifies its own violence as higher truth. At this crossroad Osama bin Laden meets Jean-Jacques Dessalines, and Vladimir Lenin meets George W. Bush. If we do not wish to go that route—and I do not—then our tools of historical mapping are in need of radical refashioning.

Avenging Angels

> "We have rendered to these true cannibals, war for war, crime for crime, outrage for outrage; yes, I have saved my country: I have avenged America."
>
> DESSALINES, 22 APRIL 1805[154]

> "Our Haitian painters depict the Deity and angels black, while they represent the devil as white."
>
> BARON DE VASTEY, 1816[155]

153. On Dessalines's slogan, see Dubois, *Avengers of the New World*. On "giving as good as he got," see Dash, "Theater of the Haitian Revolution," 19.

154. Cited in Dayan, *Haiti, History and the Gods*, 4.

155. Vastey, *Réflexions*, 22.

The Haitian Revolution is a triumph for universal history only in our imaginations. That is not insignificant. Empathic imagination may well be our best hope for humanity. The problem is that we never seem to imagine this humanity inclusively enough, but only by excluding an antithetical other, a collective enemy beyond humanity's pale. As a consequence, any political movement that attempts to transform the death's-head (the skeletal remains of the victims of history) into an angel's face (history's redeemer) is far more likely to unleash a human hell. Imagination, intending to set the world aright, makes a virtue out of violence against the violator. If enlightened critique stops here, it entrenches itself behind a self-imposed and self-defeating barrier, one that must be dismantled if humanity is to progress beyond the recurring cycle of victim and avenger.

Let us allow that the events of the Haitian Revolution cannot be contained within a tale of historical redemption—Hegelian, Marxist, Muslim, or otherwise. Indeed, viewed from the midst of the slave uprising, no clear historical narrative emerges of any kind. "[I]nter-ethnic conflict among slaves did not disappear during the Revolution."[156] The rebels were never a monolithic mass. Loyalties shifted, as British, Spanish, French-republican, and French-royalist support was sought at times by various factions during the decade-long struggle that has been described aptly as "a war within *the* war."[157] Slave leaders fought against and betrayed each other. There are recorded instances of reversion to the African precedent of bartering slaves (to the Spanish) for guns.[158] Personal trust under such conditions would have been almost impossible to maintain. The temptation to cut through the Gordian knot by resorting to political

156. Geggus, "Bois Caïman Ceremony," 51.
157. Trouillot, *Silencing the Past*, 40.
158. Fouchard, *Haitian Maroons*, 347.

abstraction—seeing all whites (or all blacks) as enemies—would have been overwhelming. The Haitian Revolution experienced all the existential uncertainties and moral ambiguities of a struggle for liberation under conditions of civil war and foreign occupation.[159]

The less we see historical actors as playing theatrically coherent roles, the more universally accessible their human dilemmas become. Perhaps the most deadly blow to imperialism would be to proclaim loyalty to the idea of universal humanity by rejecting the presumption of any political, religious, ethnic, class, or civilizational collectivity to embody this idea as its exclusive and exclusionary possession. To believe in the legitimacy of such an appropriation is political madness. The *loa* of freedom—what C. L. R. James calls the "spirit of the thing"[160]—cannot be tied down and dragged off as a war trophy, or bought by the highest bidder.

The Haitian Constitution of 1804, declaring all citizens as "black" irrespective of color or race, has been described as "a bold and ideologically fascinating initiative"[161]—fascinating, yes, but also problematic. The constitution was imagining a unity that did not exist, as was evinced by Dessalines' own assassination in 1806 by a faction of the new Haitian citizenry, and the consequent splitting of the country into two political regimes—Henri Christophe's kingdom in the north and Pétion's republic in the south (both leaders claimed the mantle of the revolution).[162] Moreover, as ideology, Haiti's black identity functioned as a national myth that was in tension with the idea of universal emancipation to which the revolution

159. That similar conditions of a "war within the war" came to exist in Iraq as a consequence of the U.S. 2003 invasion is a safe assumption.

160. James, *Black Jacobins*, 391.

161. Beckles, "'Unnatural and Dangerous Independence,'" 164.

162. To avoid the fate of Dessalines, in the midst of an uprising Christophe (King Henri I) committed suicide. See Trouillot, *Silencing the Past*, 40–69, for a careful interpretation of Christophe's reign that rejects seeing him as a "bare mimic" of European monarchs.

had given birth.[163] The Baron de Vastey, advisor and spokesperson for Christophe, echoed the words of Robert Wedderburn and Thomas Paine when he proclaimed: "the cause that I defend is that of the entirety of humanity. Whites, yellows and blacks, we are all brothers."[164] And yet when he and others produced a discourse of Haiti as a nation raising itself up to the level of European nations, the original emancipatory project wherein "national boundaries played a minor role," was transmuted into "a particularism in which national interest and respect for national boundaries took precedence."[165]

Haitians saw themselves as "a symbol of black dignity and black power" in terms that were "unambiguously ethno-national."[166] By defining Haiti vis-à-vis the enemy and arguing *within the context*

---

163. Hence, although "almost all black and coloured Haitians accepted the fact that they belonged to the black or African race," and indeed took pride in this fact of racial identity as the basis of their claim to independence, politics in Haiti was from the start "largely concerned with a struggle for power between two elite groups, designated principally by colour . . . [that] developed out of the 'caste' distinctions of colonial Saint Domingue" (Nicholls, *From Dessalines to Duvalier*, 1–2, 7.) See Fouchard's anguished critique of his nation's racism in *Haitian Maroons*, 358.

164. Vastey, *Réflexions*, 112. It was de Vastey who responded in outrage to the French discussion during the slave uprising that to uproot the idea of liberty from Saint-Domingue, it might be necessary to exterminate all of the existing slave population, and replace it with a new one within which the memory of rebellion would be eradicated: "Grand Dieu! Quelle lumière! Quelles vois pour civiliser et éclairer des hommes que celle de la traite!" (*Réflexions*, 48).

165. Fischer, *Modernity Disavowed*, 259. Commenting on the Haitian journals of these years, Nicholls describes the "somewhat ambivalent" attitude they expressed toward Africa. "While they denied vehemently any notion of the inherent inferiority of Africans, they often assumed that Africa was a barbarous continent and that the only civilization worth considering in their own day was European. 'We realize what efforts we in turn must make,' wrote King Henry [Christophe] to [the British abolitionist Thomas] Clarkson, 'in order to fulfill your hope of being some day able to raise up Africa to the level of European civilization.'" (Nicholls, *From Dessalines to Duvalier*, 42–43).

166. Nicholls, *From Dessalines to Duvalier*, 3, 41. Nicholls makes a distinction between the nineteenth century, when Haitian intellectuals, mulatto and black, "agreed that in cultural matters the European pattern of civilization was the one which Haiti should follow" (*From Dessalines to Duvalier*, 11), and the twentieth century, when ideas of negritude led to questioning the relevance of the European model altogether, and championing African identity as different and distinct.

of European civilization that "the blacks, like the whites, are men"[167] capable of founding "a civilized nation according to European standards"[168]—complete with (masculinist) military prowess, (export-oriented) commerce, (plantation) agriculture, and a monumental, royal palace (built by forced, "free" labor)—they allowed the contribution to the cause of universal humanity that emerged in this event to slip from view.[169] Haiti's political imaginary as liberated territory, a safe haven for all, was too grand for statist politics. Its absolutely new extension of both freedom and citizenship transracially and transnationally, does not lend itself to political appropriation as a definition of national identity.[170]

If we understand the experience of historical rupture as a *moment* of clarity, temporary by definition, we will not be in danger of losing the world-historical contribution of the Saint-Domingue slaves, the idea of an end to relations of slavery that went far beyond existing European Enlightenment thought—and is, indeed, far from realized under today's conditions of a global economy, where sex-slavery is rampant and the bonded labor of immigrants is employed by *all* of the so-called civilizations, and where the myth of "free

167. Christophe cited in Nicholls, *From Dessalines to Duvalier*, 42. Christophe spoke of racial differences as not intrinsically unequal but "the result of civilization and knowledge" (*From Dessalines to Duvalier*, 41).

168. Vastey, *Réflexions*, 83–84.

169. Such was Pétion's response in 1817 to the complaint that slaves had escaped to Haitian soil from a British schooner: "they are *recognized to be Haytians* by the 44th article of the constitution of the republic, from the moment they set foot in its territory, and it is out of my power to restore them to you agreeably to your demand. Each country has its own laws . . . such persons as arrive in this territory must be protected, since the laws require it . . . of the country, of which they are now citizens" (cited in Beckles, "'Unnatural and Dangerous Independence,'" 170–71). Note the echoes in Pétion's wording of legal arguments on slavery that had been made in Europe.

170. Haitian freedom extended to Indians, Poles, and others besides African blacks. We must conclude with Fischer that the conceptual locus of the idea of radical antislavery is not the nation-state (Fischer, *Modernity Disavowed*, 15). Sadly, "the disavowal of radical anti-slavery came to be constitutive for emerging national cultures in the Caribbean" as well European political discourse (*Modernity Disavowed*, 274). Compare to Trouillot: "Haiti experienced early all the trials of postcolonial nation-building" (Trouillot, *Silencing the Past*, 68).

labor" that Marx called wage-slavery is the reality for millions of members of the working class.[171] Radical antislavery is a human invention that belongs to no one, because it belongs to everyone. Such ideas are the residues of events, rather than the possession of a particular collective, and even if they fail, they can never be forgotten.

The Project of Universal History

This approach to human universality values precisely the "unhistorical histories" dismissed by Hegel, including the collective actions that appear out of order within coherent narratives of Western progress or cultural continuity, class struggle or dominant civilizations. Historical anomalies now take on central importance—for example, the fact that not only did the freed slaves resist under Toussaint's new system of "military agrarianism" when told to resume plantation labor as before, but women made the unprecedented demand of equal pay for equal work (rather than the two-thirds ratio that was considered the European, "civilized" norm), arguing that their tasks, hours, and conditions were the same as those of men. "Simply stated, the women saw themselves as individual and equal workers"—and the men did not object.[172] The French representative Poverel felt compelled to appeal to more primitive ideas of gender to convince them otherwise.[173]

171. "It is not yet time to look back to some fossilized theme of slavery, for slavery still exists under other names" (Dayan, *Haiti, History and the Gods*, 11).

172. Fick, *Making of Haiti*, 170. Fick pays attention to this demand as part of a comprehensive understanding of the idea of human freedom. The Haitian historian Fouchard also acknowledges this moment, when "Black women had the temerity to claim equal salaries with men," and criticizes the fact that "this initial feminist demand was listened to with only half an ear and drowned in considerations about inequality in physical strength" (Fouchard, *Haitian Maroons*, 223).

173. "Africans, if you want your women to listen to reason, listen to reason yourself" (Pomeral, cited in Fick, *Making of Haiti*, 171).

If on the one hand, the anomalies of the Haitian experience are seen as its progressive moments, on the other hand, the brutalities of slavery prove to be historically routine. We are obliged to attend to Métraux's comment in 1960 that "the atrocities committed on the plantations might seem incredible if Europeans themselves had not, in turn, fallen victim to the same practices under totalitarian regimes."[174] By the same token, while we may easily share Sala-Molin's moral outrage, discussed in "Hegel and Haiti," at the way European Enlightenment philosophers railed against slavery *except where it literally existed*, we cannot deny that a comparable moral outrage is occurring at this moment, one that future generations will find just as deplorable (this is our moral hope), the fact that political collectives proclaim themselves champions of human rights and the rule of law and then deny these to a whole list of enemy exceptions, as if humanity itself were the monopoly of their own privileged members—their war a just war, their terrorist acts a moral duty, their death and destruction legitimated by reason, or progress, or the divine.

Universal history engages in a double liberation, of the historical phenomena and of our own imagination: by liberating the past we liberate ourselves. The limits to our imagination need to be taken down brick by brick, chipping away at the cultural embeddedness that predetermines the meaning of the past in ways that hold us captive in the present. We exist behind cultural borders, the defense of which is a boon to politicians. The fight to free the facts from the collective histories in which they are embedded is one with exposing and expanding the porosity of a global social field, where individual experience is not so much hybrid as human. Liberation from the exclusionary loyalties of collective identities is precisely

174. Métreau, *Voodoo in Haiti*, 16.

what makes progress possible in history, which is not to say that global trade fosters understanding, peace, or universality (it connects directly with the sale of arms, the initiation of wars, and the degradation and displacement of laboring people). Instead, it is to argue that one of the feared "risks" of long-distance trade (exploited by imperialists and anti-imperialists alike) is the fear of falling off the cultural edge of one's own world and its self-understanding. This fear may one day appear as childlike and primitive as clinging to the belief that the earth is flat.

Nothing keeps history univocal except power. We will never have a definitive answer as to the intent of historical actors, and even if we could, this would not be history's truth. It is not that truth is multiple or that the truth is a whole ensemble of collective identities with partial perspectives. Truth is singular, but it is a continuous process of inquiry because it builds on a present that is moving ground. History keeps running away from us, going places we, mere humans, cannot predict. The politics of scholarship that I am suggesting is neutrality, but not of the nonpartisan, "truth lies in the middle" sort; rather, it is a *radical* neutrality that insists on the porosity of the space between enemy sides, a space contested and precarious, to be sure, but free enough for the idea of humanity to remain in view.

Between uniformity and indeterminacy of historical meaning, there is a dialectical encounter with the past. In extending the boundaries of our moral imagination, we need to *see* a historical space before we can explore it. The mutual recognition between past and present that can liberate us from the recurring cycle of victim and aggressor can occur only if the past to be recognized is on the historical map. It is in the picture, even if it is not in place. Its liberation is a task of excavation that takes place not across national boundaries, but without them. Its richest finds are at the edge of culture. Universal humanity is visible at the edges.

There is no end to this project, only an infinity of connecting links. And if these are to be connected without domination, then the links will be lateral, additive, syncretic rather than synthetic. The project of universal history does not come to an end. It begins again, somewhere else.

Adorno, Theodor W. *Negative Dialectics*. Translated by E. B. Ashton. New York: The Seabury Press, 1973.

Althaus, Horst. *Hegel und die heroischen Jahre der Philosophie: Eine Biographie*. Münich: Karl Hanser Verlag, 1992.

Anglade, Pierre. *Inventaire Etymologique des Termes Creoles des Caraibes d'Origine Africaine*. Paris: L'Harmattan, 1998.

Archenholz, Johann Wilhelm von. "Zur neuesten Geschichte von St. Domingo." *Minerva* 4 (November 1804): 340.

Arroyo, Jossianna. "Technologies: transculturations of race, gender and ethnicity in Arturo A. Schomburg's Masonic writings." *CENTRO: Journal of the Center for Puerto Rican Studies* 17, no. 1 (Spring 2005): 4–25.

Avineri, Shlomo. *Hegel's Theory of the Modern State*. Cambridge: Cambridge University Press, 1974.

Beckles, Hilary McD. "'An Unnatural and Dangerous Independence': the Haitian Revolution and the Political Sociology of Caribbean Slavery." *Journal of Caribbean Studies* 25, no. 1/2 (1991): 160–77.

Bellhouse, Mary. "Candide Shoots the Monkey Lovers: Representing Black Men in Eighteenth-Century French Visual Culture." *Political Theory* 34, no. 6 (December 2006): 741–84.

Bénot, Yves. "Comment la Convention a-t-elle voté l'abolition de l'esclavage en l'an II?" In *Révolutions aux colonies*, edited by Michel Vouvelle. Paris: Annales Historiques de la Révolution Français, 1993.

Bernasconi, Robert. "Hegel at the Court of the Ashanti." In *Hegel after Derrida*, edited by Stuart Barnett, 41–63. London: Routledge, 1998.

Blackburn, Robin. *The Overthrow of Colonial Slavery, 1776–1848*. London: Verso, 1988.

Blakeley, Allison. *Blacks in the Dutch World: The Evolution of Racial Imagery in a Modern Society*. Bloomington: Indiana University Press, 1993.

Blewett, David. *The Illustration of Robinson Crusoe, 1719–1920*. Gerrards Cross: Colin Smythe, 1995.

Blumenberg, Hans. *The Genesis of the Copernican World*. Translated by Robert M. Wallace. Cambridge: The MIT Press, 1987.

Braudel, Ferdinand. *Civilization and Capitalism, 15th–18th Century*. Vol. III, *The Perspective of the World*. Translated by Siân Reynolds. Berkeley: University of California Press, 1992.

Buck-Morss, Susan. *The Dialectics of Seeing: Walter Benjamin and the Arcades Project.* Cambridge: The MIT Press, 1989.

———. "Envisioning Capital: Political Economy on Display." *Critical Inquiry* 21, no. 2 (Winter 1995): 434–67. Reprinted in Peter Wollen, ed., *Visual Display*. New York: DIA, 1996.

———. *Explosion in a Cathedral* [El Siglo de las luces]. Translated by John Sturrock. New York: Harper & Row, 1963.

Cauna, Jacques de. "Polverel et Sonthonax, deux voies pour l'abolition de l'esclavage." In *Léger-Félicité Sonthonax: La première abolition de l'esclavage; La Révolution française et la Révolution de Saint-Domingue*, edited by Marcel Dorigny, 49–53. Saint-Denis: Société française d'histoire d'outre-mer, 1997.

Césaire, Aimé. *Toussaint Louverture: La Révolution française et le problème colonial*. Paris: Présence africaine, 1960.

Clawson, Mary Ann. *Constructing Brotherhood: Class, Gender and Fraternalism*. Princeton: Princeton University Press, 1989.

Cohen, William B. *The French Encounter with the Africans: White Response to Blacks 1530–1880*. Bloomington: Indiana University Press, 1980.

Curl, James Stevens. *The Art and Architecture of Freemasonry: An Introductory Study*. London: B.T. Batsford, 1991.

Dabydeen, David. *Hogarth's Blacks: Images of Blacks in Eighteenth Century English Art*. Athens: University of Georgia Press, 1987.

Dash, J. Michael. "Le Je de l'autre." *L'Esprit Créateur* 47, no. 1 (2007): 84–95.

———. "The Theater of the Haitian Revolution and the Haitian Revolution as Theater." *Small Axe* 18 (Sept. 2005): 16–23.

Davis, David Brion. *The Problem of Slavery in the Age of Revolution, 1770–1823*. Ithaca: Cornell University Press, 1975.

———. *The Problem of Slavery in Western Culture*. Ithaca: Cornell University Press, 1966.

———. *Revolutions: Reflections on American Equality and Foreign Liberations*. Cambridge: Harvard University Press, 1990.

———. "Slavery—White, Black, Muslim, and Christian." *New York Review of Books*, vol. 48, no. 11 (July 5, 2001). http://www.nybooks.com/articles/ 14320.

Davis, Ralph. *The Rise of the Atlantic Economies*. Ithaca: Cornell University Press, 1973.

Dayan, Joan. *Haiti, History and the Gods*. Berkeley: University of California Press, 1995.

———. "Paul Gilroy's Slaves, Ships, and Routes: The Middle Passage as Metaphor." *Research in African Literatures* 27, no. 4 (Winter 1996): 7–14.

Debien, Gabriel. *Les Esclaves aux Antilles français (XVIIe–XVIIIe siècles)*. Abasse-Terre, Guadaloupe: Société d'Histoire de la Guadaloupe, 1974.

Denslow, William R. *Freemasonry and the American Indian*. St. Louis: Missouri Lodge of Research, 1956.

Desmangles, Leslie G. *The Faces of God: Vodou and Roman Catholicism in Haiti*. Chapel Hill: University of North Carolina Press, 1992.

Desné, Roland. "Sonthonax vu par les dictionnaires." In *Léger-Félicité Sonthonax: La première abolition de l'esclavage; La Révolution française et la Révolution de Saint-Domingue*, edited by Marcel Dorigny, 113–20. Saint-Denis: Société française d'histoire d'outre-mer, 1997.

Diderot, Denis, Jean le Rond d'Alembert, and Pierre Mouchon. *Encyclopédie, ou, Dictionnaire raisonné de sciences, artes et des métiers*. 34 vols. Stuttgart-Bad Cannstatt: Frommann, 1966–1995. Originally published in Paris: Briasson, 1751–1780.

Diouf, Sylviane A. *Servants of Allah: African Muslims Enslaved in the Americas*. New York: New York University Press, 1998.

Dorigny, Marcel, ed. *Léger-Félicité Sonthonax: La première abolition de l'esclavage; La Révolution française et la Révolution de Saint-Domingue*. Saint-Denis: Société française d'histoire d'outre-mer, 1997.

Dubois, Laurent. *Avengers of the New World: The Story of the Haitian Revolution*. Cambridge: Harvard University Press, 2004.

———. *A Colony of Citizens: Revolution and Slave Emancipation in the French Caribbean, 1787–1804*. Chapel Hill: University of North Carolina Press, 2004.

———. "Inscribing Race in the Revolutionary French Antilles." In *The Color of Liberty: Histories of Race in France*, edited by Sue Peabody and Tyler Stovall. Durham: Duke University Press, 2003.

DuBois, W. E. B. *Black Reconstruction in America: An Essay Toward a History of the Part Which Black Folk Played in the Attempt to Reconstruct Democracy in America, 1860–1880*. New York: Atheneum, 1977.

Dupuy, Alex. *Haiti in the World Economy: Class, Race, and Underdevelopment since 1700*. Boulder: Westview Press, 1989.

Fanon, Frantz. *The Wretched of the Earth*. Translated by Constance Farrington. New York: Grove Press, 1968.

Farnie, D. A. *The English Cotton Industry and the World Market*. Oxford: Clarendon Press, 1979.

Faÿ, Bernard. *Revolution and Freemasonry, 1680–1800*. Boston: Little, Brown, and Company, 1935.

Federici, Silvia. *Caliban and the Witch: Women, the Body and Primitive Accumulation*. Brooklyn: Autonomedia, 2004.

Fick, Carolyn E. "The French Revolution in Saint Domingue: A Triumph or a Failure?" In *A Turbulent Time: The French Revolution and the Greater Caribbean*, edited by David Barry Gaspar and David Patrick Geggus. Bloomington: Indiana University Press, 1997.

———. *The Making of Haiti: The Saint Domingue Revolution from Below*. Knoxville: University of Tennessee Press, 1990.

———. "The Saint Domingue Slave Insurrection of 1791." *Journal of Caribbean History* 25, no. 1/2 (1991): 1–40.

Fischer, Sibylle. *Modernity Disavowed: Haiti and the Cultures of Slaves in The Age of Revolution*. Durham: Duke University Press, 2004.

Forster, Michael N. *Hegel's Idea of a Phenomenology of Spirit*. Chicago: University of Chicago Press, 1998.

Fouchard, Jean. *The Haitian Maroons: Liberty or Death*. Translated by A. Faulkner Watts. Preface by C. L. R. James. New York: Edward W. Blyden Press, 1981.

Geggus, David Patrick. "The Bois Caïman Ceremony." *Journal of Caribbean History* 25, no. 1/2 (1991): 41–57.

———. "British Occupation of Saint Domingue, 1793–98." PhD diss., York University, England, 1978.

———. "British Opinion and the Emergence of Haiti, 1791–1805." In *Slavery and British Society, 1776–1846,* edited by James Walvin. Baton Rouge: Louisiana State University, 1982.

———. "From His Most Catholic Majesty to the Godless Republique: The 'Volte-Face' of Toussaint Louverture and the End of Slavery in Saint Domingue." *Revue française d'histoire d'outre mer* 65, no. 241 (1978): 481–99. Reprinted in Paris: Société française d'histoire d'outre-mer, 1997.

———. "Haiti and the Abolitionists: Opinion, Propaganda, and International Politics in Britain and France, 1804–1838." In *Abolition and Its Aftermath: The Historical Context, 1790–1916*, edited by David Richardson. London: Frank Cass, 1985.

———. *Haitian Revolutionary Studies*. Bloomington: Indiana University Press, 2002.

———. "Slavery, War, and Revolution in the Greater Caribbean." In *A Turbulent Time: The French Revolution and the Greater Caribbean*, edited by David Barry Gaspar and David Patrick Geggus. Bloomington: Indiana University Press, 1997.

Genovese, Eugene D. *The Political Economy of Slavery: Studies in the Economy and Society of the Slave South*. New York: Vintage Books, 1965.

_____. *Rebellion to Revolution: Afro-American Slave Revolts and the Making of the Modern World*. Baton Rouge: Louisiana State University Press, 1979.

Gilroy, Paul. *The Black Atlantic: Modernity and Double Consciousness*. Cambridge: Harvard University Press, 1993.

Gomez, Michael A. *Black Crescent: The Experience and Legacy of African Muslims in the Americas*. New York: Cambridge University Press, 2005.

Gooch, G. P. *Germany and the French Revolution*. New York: Longmans, Green and Co., 1920.

Guha, Ranajit. *History at the Limit of World History*. New York: Columbia University Press, 2002.

Guietti, Paolo. "A Reading of Hegel's Master/Slave Relationship: Robinson Crusoe and Friday." *Owl of Minerva* 25, no. 1 (Fall 1993): 48–60.

Habermas, Jürgen. *The Philosophical Discourse of Modernity*. Cambridge: The MIT Press, 1987.

_____. *The Structural Transformation of the Public Sphere: An Inquiry into a Category of Bourgeois Society*. Translated by Thomas Burger and Frederick Lawrence. Cambridge: The MIT Press, 1989.

Hall, Nevill A. T. *Slave Society in the Danish West Indies, St. Thomas, St. John, and St. Croix*. Baltimore: The Johns Hopkins University Press, 1992.

Harris, Henry S. "The Concept of Recognition in Hegel's Jena Manuscripts." In *Hegel Studien/Beiheft 20: Hegel in Jena*, edited by Dieter Henrich and Klaus Düsing. Bonn: Bouvier, 1980.

Haym, Rudolf. *Hegel und seine Zeit: Vorlesungen über Entstehung und Entwicklung, Wesen und Wert der Hegelschen Philosophie*. Berlin: Rudolph Gärtner, 1857.

Hegel, Georg Wilhelm Frederich. *Briefe von und an Hegel*. Edited by Johannes Hoffmeister. Hamburg: Felix Meiner Verlag, 1969–1981.

_____. *Early Theological Writings*. Translated and edited by T. M. Knox. Chicago: University of Chicago Press, 1948.

_____. *The Encyclopaedia Logic (with the Zusätze)*. Translated and edited by T. F. Geraets, W. A. Suchting, and H. S. Harris. Indianapolis: Hackett Publishing Company, 1991.

_____. *Gesammelte Werke*. Edited under the direction of the German Research Association. Hamburg: Felix Meiner Verlag, 1968–.

_____. *Hegel, The Letters*. Translated by Clark Butler and Christiane Seiler. Bloomington: Indiana University Press, 1984.

_____. *Jenaer Systementwürfe I: Das System der spekulativen Philosophie*. Edited by Klaus Düsing and Heinz Kimmerle. Hamburg: Felix Meiner Verlag, 1986.

_____. *Jenaer Systementwürfe II. Logik, Metaphysik, Naturphilosophie*. Edited by Rolf-Peter Horstmann and Johann Heinrich Trede. Hamburg: Felix Meiner Verlag, 1982.

——. *Jenaer Systementwürfe III: Naturphilosophie und Philosophie des Geistes*. Edited by Rolf-Peter Horstmann. Hamburg: Felix Meiner Verlag, 1987.

——. *The Phenomenology of Mind*. Translated by J. B. Baille. New York: Harper & Row, 1967.

——. *The Philosophical Propaedeutic*. Translated by A. V. Miller. Edited by Michael George and Andrew Vincent. Oxford: Oxford University Press, 1986.

——. *Die Philosophie des Rechts: Die Mitschriften Wannenmann (Heidelberg 1817/18) und Homeyer (Berlin 1818/19)*. Edited by Karl-Heinz Ilting. Stuttgart: Klett-Cotta, 1983.

——. *The Philosophy of History*. Translated by John Sibree. Buffalo: Prometheus Books, 1991.

——. *Philosophy of Right*. Translated and edited by T. M. Knox. London: Oxford University Press, 1967.

——. *Philosophy of Subjective Spirit*. 3 vols. Translated and edited by M. J. Petry. Dordrecht: D. Reidel Publishing Co., 1979.

——. *Sämtliche Werke*. Vol. 10, *System der Philosophie: Dritter Teil. Die Philosophie des Geistes*. Edited by Hermann Glockner. Stuttgart: Fr. Frommanns Verlag, 1958.

——. *System of Ethical Life (1802/3) and First Philosophy of Spirit (Part III of the System of Speculative Philosophy 1803/4)*. Translated and edited by H. S. Harris and T. M. Knox. Albany: State University of New York Press, 1979.

——. *System der Sittlichkeit*. Edited by Georg Lasson [1923]. Hamburg: Felix Meiner Verlag, 1967.

——. *Die Vernunft in der Geschichte*. 5th edition. Edited by Johannes Hoffmeister. Hamburg: Verlag von Felix Meiner, 1955.

——. *Vorlesungen über die Philosophie der Weltgeschichte*. 3 vols. Edited by Karl Heinz Ilting, Karl Brehmer, and Hoo Nam Seelmann. Hamburg: Felix Meiner Verlag, 1996.

Herskovits, Melville J. *Dahomey, an Ancient West African Kingdom*. New York: J. J. Augustin, Publisher, 1938.

Hondt, Jacques d'. *Hegel et les Français*. Hildesheim: Georg Olms Verlag, 1998.

——. *Hegel Secret: Recherches sur les sources cachées de la pensée de Hegel*. Paris: Presses Universitaires de France, 1968.

Honneth, Axel. *The Struggle for Recognition: The Moral Grammar of Social Conflicts*. Translated by Joel Anderson. Cambridge: Polity Press, 1995.

Honour, Hugh. *From the American Revolution to World War I*. Vol. 4 of *The Image of the Black in Western Art*, edited by Ladislas Bugner. Cambridge: Harvard University Press, 1989.

Hulme, Peter. "The Spontaneous Hand of Nature: Savagery, Colonialism, and the Enlightenment." In *The Enlightenment and Its Shadows*, edited by Peter Hulme and Ludmilla Jordanova. London: Routledge, 1990.

Huntington, Samuel P. *The Clash of Civilizations and the Remaking of World Order*. New York: Simon & Schuster, 1997.

Hutin, Serge. *Les Francs-Maçons*. Paris: Éditions du Seuil, 1960.

Hyppolite, Jean. *Genesis and Structure of Hegel's "Phenomenology of Spirit."* Translated by Samuel Chernak and John Heckman. Evanston: Northwestern University Press, 1974.

James, C. L. R. *The Black Jacobins: Toussaint L'Ouverture and the San Domingo Revolution*. New York: Vintage Books, 1963.

Janzen, John M. *Lemba, 1650–1930: A Drum of Affliction in Africa and the New World*. New York: Garland Publishing, 1982.

Jordan, Winthrop D. *White Over Black: American Attitudes toward the Negro, 1550–1812*. Chapel Hill: University of North Carolina Press, 1968.

Kant, Immanuel. "The Contest of Faculties." In *Kant's Political Writings*, edited by Hans Reiss. Translated by H. B. Nisbet. Cambridge: Cambridge University Press, 1970.

———. *Critique of Practical Reason*. Translated by Werner S. Pluhar. Indianapolis: Hackett Publishing Company, 2002.

Kelley, George Armstrong. "Notes on Hegel's 'Lordship and Bondage.'" In *Dialectic of Desire and Recognition: Texts and Commentary*, edited by John O'Neill. Albany: State University of New York Press, 1996.

Kojève, Alexandre. *Introduction to the Reading of Hegel: Lectures on the Phenomenology of Spirit*. Assembled by Raymond Queneau. Edited by Allan Bloom. Translated by James H. Nichols Jr. Ithaca: Cornell University Press, 1969.

Landon, H. C. Robbins. *Mozart and the Masons: New Light on the Lodge of "Crowned Hope."* London: Thames & Hudson, 1982.

Lewis, David Levering. "Introduction." In *W. E. B. Dubois: A Reader*, edited by David Levering Lewis. New York: Holt, 1995.

Linebaugh, Peter. *The London Hanged: Crime and Civil Society in the Eighteenth Century*. New York: Cambridge University Press, 1992.

Linebaugh, Peter, and Marcus Rediker. *The Many-Headed Hydra: Sailors, Slaves, Commoners, and the Hidden History of the Revolutionary Atlantic*. Boston: Beacon Press, 2000.

Lipson, Dorothy Ann. *Freemasonry in Federalist Connecticut*. Princeton: Princeton University Press, 1977.

Lloyd-Jones, Roger, and M. J. Lewis. *Manchester and the Age of the Factory: The Business Structure of Cottonopolis in the Industrial Revolution*. London: Croom Helm, 1988.

Locke, John. *Two Treatises of Government*. Edited by Peter Laslett. Cambridge: Cambridge University Press, 1960.

Lukács, George. *Der junge Hegel: Über die Beziehungen von Dialektik und Ökonomie*. Zürich: Europa Verlag, 1948.

Marcuse, Herbert. *Reason and Revolution: Hegel and the Rise of Social Theory*. London: Oxford University Press, 1941.

Matory, J. Lorand. "The English Professors of Brazil: On the Diasporic Roots of the Yorùbá Nation." *Society for Comparative Study of Society and History* (1999):72–103.

Mehta, Uday S. "Liberal Strategies of Exclusion." *Politics and Society* 18 (December 1990): 427–53.

Meillassoux, Claude. *The Anthropology of Slavery: The Womb of Iron and Gold*. Translated by Alide Dasnois. Chicago: University of Chicago Press, 1991.

Métraux, Alfred. *Voodoo in Haiti*. Translated by Hugo Charteris. New York: Oxford University Press, 1959.

Mignolo, Walter D. *The Darker Side of the Renaissance: Literacy, Territoriality, and Colonialization*. Ann Arbor: University of Michigan Press, 2003.

Mintz, Sidney W. *Sweetness and Power: The Place of Sugar in Modern History*. New York: Penguin Books, 1985.

Montag, Warren. *Bodies, Masses, Power: Spinoza and His Contemporaries*. London: Verso, 1999.

Montesquieu. "The Spirit of the Laws." In *Selected Political Writings*. Edited and translated by Melvin Richter. Indianapolis: Hackett Publishing Company, 1990.

Muthu, Sankar. *Enlightenment Against Empire*. Princeton: Princeton University Press, 2003.

Nesbitt, Nick. "Troping Toussaint, Reading Revolution." *Research in African Literatures* 35, no. 2 (Summer 2004): 18–33.

———. *Voicing Memory: History and Subjectivity in French Caribbean Literature*. Charlottesville: University of Virginia Press, 2003.

Nicholls, David. *From Dessalines to Duvalier: Race, Colour and National Independence in Haiti*. Cambridge: Cambridge University Press, 1979.

Noerr, Gunzelin Schmid. *Sinnlichkeit und Herrchaft: Zur Konzeptiualisierung der inneren Natur bei Hegel und Freud*. Königstein/Taunus: Verlag Anton Hain, 1980.

Oelsner, Konrad Engelbert. *Luzifer oder gereinigte Beiträge zur Geschichte der Französischen Revolution*. Edited by Jörn Garber. Kronberg/Taunus: Scriptor Verlag, 1997.

O'Neill, John, ed. *Hegel's Dialectic of Desire and Recognition*. Albany: State University of New York, 1996.

Pachonski, Jan, and Reuel K. Wilson. *Poland's Caribbean Tragedy: A Study of Polish Legions in the Haitian War of Independence, 1802–3*. New York: Columbia University Press, 1986.

Palmer, R. R., and Joel Colton. *A History of the Modern World*. New York: Alfred A. Knopf, 1969.

Palmié, Stephan. *Wizards and Scientists: Explorations in Afro-Cuban Modernity and Tradition*. Durham: Duke University Press, 2002.

Patterson, Orlando. *Slavery and Social Death: A Comparative Study*. Cambridge: Harvard University Press, 1982.

Paulson, Ronald. *Representations of Revolution (1789–1820)*. New Haven: Yale University Press, 1983.

Peabody, Sue. *"There Are No Slaves in France": The Political Culture of Race and Slavery in the Ancien Régime*. New York: Oxford University Press, 1996.

Peabody, Sue, and Tyler Stovall, eds. *The Color of Liberty: Histories of Race in France*. Durham: Duke University Press, 2003.

Petry, M. J. "Hegel and 'The Morning Chronicle.'" *Hegel-Studien* 11 (1976): 11–80.

Pinkard, Terry. *Hegel: A Biography*. Cambridge: Cambridge University Press, 2000.

Pöggeler, Otto. *Hegels Idee einer Phänomenologie des Geistes*. Freiburg: Verlag Karl Alber, 1993.

Rae, John. *Life of Adam Smith*. New York: Augustus M. Kelley, 1965.

Rainsford, Marcus. *An Historical Account of the Black Empire of Hayti*. London: Albion Press, 1805.

———. "Toussaint-Louverture. Eine historische Schilderung für die Nachwelt." *Minerva* 56 (1805): 276–98, 392–408.

Rediker, Marcus, Peter Linebaugh, and David Brion Davis. "'The Many-Headed Hydra': An exchange." *New York Review of Books*, vol. 48, no. 14 (September 20, 2001), http://www.nybooks.com/articles/14534.

Réis, João José. *Slave Rebellion in Brazil: The 1835 Muslim Uprising in Bahia*. Translated by Arthur Brakel. Baltimore: The Johns Hopkins Press, 1995.

Riedel, Manfred. *Between Tradition and Revolution: The Hegelian Transformation of Political Philosophy*. Translated by Walter Wright. New York: Cambridge University Press, 1984.

———. "Bürger." In *Geschichtliche Grundbegriffe: Historisches Lexikon zur politisch-sozialen Sprache in Deutschland*. Vol. 1. Edited by Otto Brunner, Werner Conze, and Reinhart Koselleck. Stuttgart: Ernst Klett Verlag, 1972.

Rieger, Ute. *Johann Wilhelm von Archenholz als "Zeitbürger": Eine historisch-analytische Untersuchung zur Aufklärung*. Berlin: Duncker & Humblot, 1994.

Ritter, Joachim. *Hegel and the French Revolution: Essays on the Philosophy of Right*. Translated with an introduction by Richard Dien Winfield. Cambridge: The MIT Press, 1982.

Roberts, J. M. *The Mythology of the Secret Societies*. New York: Charles Scribner's Sons, 1972.

Robinson, Cedric J. *Black Marxism: The Making of the Black Radical Tradition*. London: Zed Books, 1983.

Rosenkranz, Karl. *Georg Wilhelm Friedrich Hegels Leben*. Darmstadt: Wissenschaftliche Buchgesellschaft, 1977.

Rousseau, Jean-Jacques. *The Basic Political Writings*. Edited and translated by Donald A. Cress. Indianapolis: Hackett Publishing Company, 1988.

Ruof, Friedrich. *Johann Wilhelm von Archenholtz: Ein deutscher Schriftsteller zur Zeit der Französischen Revolution und Napoleons (1741–1812)*. Vaduz: Kraus Reprint Ltd., 1965.

Saine, Thomas P. *Black Bread—White Bread: German Intellectuals and the French Revolution*. Columbia: Camden House, 1988.

Sala-Molins, Louis. *L'Afrique aux Amériques: Le Code Noir espangnol*. Paris: Presses Universitaires de France, 1992.

———. *Le Code Noire, ou le calvaire de Canaan*. Paris: Presses Universitaires de France, 1987.

Saugera, Eric. *Bordeaux, port négrier: chronologie, économie, idéologie, XVIIe–XIXe siècles*. Paris: Karthala, 1995.

Schama, Simon. *The Embarrassment of Riches: An Interpretation of Dutch Culture in the Golden Age*. New York: Alfred A. Knopf, 1987.

Schmitt, Carl. *Political Theology: Four Chapters on the Concept of Sovereignty*. Translated by Tracy B. Strong. Chicago: University of Chicago Press, 2005.

Schüller, Karin. *Die deutsche Rezeption haitianischer Geschichte in der ersten Hälfte des 19. Jahrhunderts, ein Beitrag zum deutschen Bild vom Schwarzen*. Cologne: Böhlau Verlag, 1992.

Shklar, Judith N. "Self-Sufficient Man: Domination and Bondage." In *Hegel's Dialectic of Desire and Recognition*, edited by John O'Neill. Albany: State University of New York, 1996.

Shyllon, F. O. *Black Slaves in Britain*. New York: Oxford University Press, 1974.

Siep, Ludwig. *Anerkennung als Prinzip der praktische Philosophie: Untersuchungen zur Hegels Jenaer Philosophie des Geistes*. Freiburg: Alber Verlag, 1978.

———. "Kampf um Anerkennung: Zu Hegels Auseinandersetzung mit Hobbes in den Jenaer Schriften." *Hegel-Studien* 9. Bonn: Bouvier Verlag, 1974. Reprinted as "The Struggle for Recognition: Hegel's Dispute with Hobbes in the Jena Writings." In *Hegel's Dialectic of Desire and Recognition*, edited by John O'Neill. Translated by Charles Dudas. Albany: State University of New York, 1996.

Smith, Adam. *An Inquiry into the Nature and Causes of the Wealth of Nations*. Homewood: The Dorsey Press, 1979.

———. *The Wealth of Nations: Books I–III*. With introduction by Andrew Skinner. London: Penguin Books, 1970.

Sobel, Dava. *Longitude: The Story of a Lone Genius Who Solved the Greatest Scientific Problem of His Time*. New York: Penguin Books, 1995.

Tavarès, Pierre-Franklin. "La Conception de l'Afrique de Hegel comme critique." *Chemins Critiques* 2, no. 2 (September 1991): 153–66.

———. "Hegel, critique de l'Afrique, thés de Doctorat." PhD diss., Sorbonne Paris-I, Paris 1989.

———. "Hegel et Haïti ou le silence de Hegel sur Saint-Domingue." *Chemins Critiques* 2, no. 3 (May 1992): 113–31.

———. "Hegel et l'abbé Grégoire ou Question noire et Révolution Française." In *Révolutions aux colonies: Publication Des Annales Historiques De La Révolution Française*, 155–73. Paris: Société Des Etudes Robespierristes, 1993.

———. "Hegel, philosophe anti-esclavagiste, ou: Le jeune Hegel, lecteur de l'abbé Raynal." Lecture delivered at the *Conférence au Collège de France*. January 1996.

Thibau, Jacques. "Saint-Domingue á l'arrivée de Sonthonax." In *Léger-Félicité Sonthonax: La première abolition de l'esclavage; La Révolution française et la Révolution de Saint-Domingue*, edited by Marcel Dorigny. Saint-Denis: Société française d'histoire d'outre-mer, 1997.

Thompson, Robert Farris. *Flash of the Spirit: African and Afro-American Art and Philosophy*. New York: Vintage Books, 1984.

———. "The Flash of the Spirit: Haiti's Africanizing Vodun Art." In *Haitian Art*, edited by Ute Stebich. New York: H. N. Abrams, 1978.

Thornton, John K. "African Soldiers in the Haitian Revolution." *Journal of Caribbean History* 25, no. 1/2 (1991): 58–80.

———. "'I am the Subject of the King of Congo': African Political Ideology and the Haitian Revolution." *Journal of World History* 4, no. 2 (Fall 1993): 181–214.

Trouillot, Michel-Rolph. *Silencing the Past: Power and the Production of History*. Boston: Beacon Press, 1995.

Vastey, Le Baron de. *Réflexions sur une Lettre de Mazéres, ex-Colon Français, adressée à M. J.C.L. Sisomonde de Sismondi sur les Noirs et les Blancs*. Cap-Henry: Chez P. Roux, 1816.

Waszek, Norbert. "Hegels Exzerpte aus der 'Edinburgh Review' 1817–1819." *Hegel-Studien*, 20 (1985): 79–112.

———. *The Scottish Enlightenment and Hegel's Account of Civil Society*. Boston: Kluwer Academic Publishers, 1988.

Williams, Eric. *Capitalism & Slavery*. Chapel Hill: University of North Carolina Press, 1994.

Williams, Robert R. *Hegel's Ethics of Recognition*. Berkeley: University of California Press, 1997.

Williamson, Joel. *The Crucible of Race: Black-White Relations in the American South since Emancipation*. New York: Oxford University Press, 1984.

Wolf, Eric W. *Europe and the People Without History*. Berkeley: University of California Press, 1982.

Zamir, Shamoon. *Dark Voices: W. E. B. Du Bois and American Thought, 1888–1903*. Chicago: Chicago University Press, 1995.

Ziesche, Eva, and Dierk Schnitger. *Der Handschriftliche Nachlass Georg Wilhelm Friedrich Hegels und die Hegel-Bestände der Staatsbibliothek zu Berlin Preussischer Kulturbesitz*. 2 vols. Wiesbaden: Harrassowitz, 1995.